T0194222

Christians and Muslims

From History to Healing

Kenneth B. Cragg

iUniverse, Inc.
Bloomington

Christians and Muslims
From History to Healing

All Bible quotations are taken from New Revised Standard Version Bible, *copyright 1989, Division of Christian Education of the National Council of the Churches of Christ in the United States of America. Used by permission. All rights reserved.*

iUniverse books may be ordered through booksellers or by contacting:

iUniverse
1663 Liberty Drive
Bloomington, IN 47403
www.iuniverse.com
1-800-Authors (1-800-288-4677)

Because of the dynamic nature of the Internet, any web addresses or links contained in this book may have changed since publication and may no longer be valid. The views expressed in this work are solely those of the author and do not necessarily reflect the views of the publisher, and the publisher hereby disclaims any responsibility for them.

Any people depicted in stock imagery provided by Thinkstock are models, and such images are being used for illustrative purposes only.

Certain stock imagery © Thinkstock.

ISBN: 978-1-4502-8519-3 (sc)
ISBN: 978-1-4502-8520-9 (dj)
ISBN: 978-1-4502-8521-6 (ebk)

Library of Congress Control Number: 2011900427

Printed in the United States of America

iUniverse rev. date: 4/13/2011

Blessed are the peacemakers, for they will be called children of God.
—The Beatitudes of Jesus (Matthew 5:9)

Contents

Foreword

Bishop A. Kenneth Cragg

Kenneth Cragg commending Kenneth Cragg might seem an act of wayward self-congratulation were it not for the fact that the wide Atlantic stretches between us. It is not geography that has brought us into welcome contact; rather, it is mutual concern with Islam. I am A. Kenneth Cragg, and he is Kenneth B. Cragg. He employs his beta while I normally dispense with my alpha.

Our nexus is the Qur'an, the mosque, and the contemporary Islamic crisis. Such suffices to explain how AKC can be invited to write a foreword for this work of KBC. It's a happy task. *Christians and Muslims: From History to Healing* is written with an honest clarity and develops its case with perception and hope.

It is now more than seventy years since I bought my first Arabic grammar and began, shortly after, a direct, local encounter with Muslim faith and society in the Arab East—an acquaintance that was later expanded into the Indian sub-continent, the Gulf States, and North Africa.

It is evident enough from the Meccan Surahs of the Qur'an that the world needs a coexistent Islam, compatible with non-Islam. There is no doubting the priority; Muhammad was clearly told, "Your sole liability is the message you have to tell (Ma aleika illa-l-Balagh)." It may have needed then the post-Hijrah sanction of force, but not now in the global community of nations. By dint of the solidarity and habituation that its "Pillars" of religion inform and transact, the Qur'an's doctrine of human Khilafah, or "entrustment" of the good earth to the comity of peoples, can educate and enjoin a true custody of the environment and a global ethic of necessary peace.

But this Meccan priority has to restrain the Medinan power equation when it presumes to violate the worth and sanctity of any and every human life as affirmed by the Talmud and the Qur'an alike. Outside the great mosque in Lahore is a modest commemoration of the poet-philosopher, Muhammad Iqbal, the ideological "patron saint" of Pakistan. In four languages, the inscription reads, "Do they not reflect upon the Qur'an, or do their hearts have locks upon them?" (Surah 47:24).

The hope for any religion is in due self-interrogation.

Preface

The Sunday after September 11, 2001, I worshipped as usual at my church, located directly across the street from a Muslim mosque. In a remarkable gesture of good will, members of the mosque invited our congregation to an open house and an introduction to Islam. As amazing as it seems now, our Christian and Muslim communities had never met. In tragic paradox, 9/11 opened the door to dialogue.

The courageous gesture of the Muslim invitation was in stark contrast to my own uncertain feelings as a committed Christian. I had so many questions: How are Muslims different from Christians? Is Islam a peaceful or a radical religion? Is it possible for the followers of Jesus and Muhammad to find common ground?

My search for answers has motivated me to write this book. Actually, "motivated" is too mild a word. My search for answers has resulted in a passion to share my discoveries with others, because in our highly charged world, ignorance too often leads to violence and death.

As I entered the mosque that stressful Sunday, I realized that all of my religious education and travel had left me incredibly ignorant about the second largest faith in the world—Islam. Perhaps more to the point, I was ignorant of a religion that was now being labeled "the enemy." That Sunday, the people of the mosque were wonderfully gracious; I was the one in stress.

My level of ignorance on that post-9/11 Sunday is an all-too-common condition across our society, a condition that unfortunately compounds the danger to our country and encourages misunderstanding and stress in our multi-ethnic, religiously diverse nation. We pride ourselves on being a democratic nation that welcomes law-abiding people from across the world. That cause for pride is now under threat.

As I began my conscious quest for information, there were some obvious opportunities for growth close at hand. My residential community includes an acknowledged Muslim leader from Egypt who, I am proud to say, is a consultant for this book. Our larger community here in the Lehigh Valley of eastern Pennsylvania includes Muslim mosques. An active community center run by Turkish expatriates offers classes and seeks opportunities for dialogue, encouraging understanding and community solidarity. An adjacent Presbyterian church hosts a thriving, Arabic-speaking congregation.

I had been blind to the obvious, as well as ignorant of the religious challenge and risk within my world. Perhaps more embarrassing, I had never held a deep, meaningful conversation with a Muslim, even though twice I had traveled to Muslim countries. As a Christian, committed to witness for Christ, my blindness and ignorance were inexcusable.

This book chronicles my journey of awakening to the reality around me. Along the way, I have encountered the spiritual richness and complexity of Islam, the frequent misunderstanding and confusion between Islam and Christianity, and the spiritual tension between my total commitment to Jesus Christ and my seeking a sincere openness to Judaism and Islam. My steps are shadowed by apprehension over the ongoing danger of the radical terrorist movement.

My search involves exploring and acknowledging these and other contradictions. In the process, I am slowly uncovering a multi-dimensional, Christian response model intended to open discussion and lead us all (you and your congregation as well as diverse readers from across the world) into a more dynamic faith adventure. The truth of the matter is amazing and wonderful: Jesus and Muhammad, although very different, have much in common. Sharing their spiritual quest can deepen and expand our own faith commitment while leading us into a meaningful approach to international peace.

I believe that the biblical principle of loving affirmation, illustrated by the practice of our Lord, must guide us in our contacts with Muslim people. It is in this spirit that I share the concepts of true Islam as well as the sharply contrasting concepts of the radical terrorists. The information about each of these groups is information they give about themselves. It is important to note that the information about Islam is shared objectively with no intent to either affirm or discredit the Islamic faith. The same is true about information regarding the radical position—as far as possible, it is offered objectively, without a value judgment. True Islam and the radical position are often confused and joined together in popular thought. We will study both on their own terms so we can clearly recognize them for what they see themselves to be, either friend or enemy.

The search for truth often begins with confusion, and it is in the midst of the world's confusion that God challenges his people to live and serve. As you read this book, I invite you to pray with me that God will give us his vision. Then, despite fear or confusion, may we respond with humility and courage, committed to God's loving design for our community and our world.

As you reflect on my early failure and ignorance about Islam, you may find yourself in a similar state of uncertainty. Prayer and study are a wise response to life's uncertainties; however, actual hands-on participation in an area of service is the most effective way to discover what God is up to in the world around us. For some of us, the "foreign mission field" is our own community, where we may serve others, including those in poverty, undocumented aliens, or street kids living down the block. As we are open to our neighbors' needs, God opens his wisdom to us and gives us eyes to see and sensitive spirits to discern where he can creatively use us.

An Initial Glimpse of Islam

As one of the great historical faith traditions, Islam is a highly complex spiritual, moral, and political force influencing over 1.3 billion people across the globe. It is one of the three monotheistic faiths that swept out of the ancient Middle East and established itself as a major influence in the formation of human civilization. Judaism, Christianity, and Islam all accept the God of Abraham, Ishmael, Isaac, and Jacob. All accept the God of the prophets and accept as well the ethical system given on Mount Sinai to Moses. These three monotheistic faiths affirm the moral accountability of mankind, which will be judged at the final day to determine our eternal destiny in heaven or hell. All three believe in the validity of the Old Testament. Islam also believes that Jesus was born of the Virgin Mary and is the Messiah promised to the Jews.

Yet even with all these things in common, these three faith traditions have often been in major conflict. Today is different only in that the weapons of conflict in this age have the potential to destroy us all. In this time of danger, may we humbly open ourselves to God's love and seek his mercy and peace.

Our goal here is to offer a broad sweep of factual information from both a Christian and an Islamic perspective. This will prepare Christians to build relationships with Muslims in our communities. Our challenge is very similar to the initial challenge of a foreign missionary. First, we must build a relational base with the people around us; we listen and interact, continuing to understand and appreciate their perception of life. It is then that valid dialogue can occur, fuller inner awareness can develop and, God willing, a new faith community will come into being.

Although there is a wide variety of acknowledged Muslim groups, Islam primarily includes Sunni and Shiite perceptions. In sharp contrast to these truly moderate Muslim groups are purist groups such as the Wahhabi and the Muslim Brotherhood, which hold varied radical, militant ideological orientations. Since the radicals (mistakenly referred to as jihadists, which has a different Arabic meaning) have received tremendous publicity since 9/11, many people assume that they represent the majority of the Muslim population. Thus, a second goal of the book is to discredit this false view and carefully document the distinction between true Islam and terrorism, especially as seen in al Qaeda.

Our ability to counter terrorism is dependent in part on our capacity to identify the ideology of true Islam and to be aware of its goals. Then we can correctly identify the contrasting terrorist position. As our understanding increases, we will be in a much stronger position to live out our faith and safeguard the peace and integrity of our freedom. In simple terms, valid counter-terrorism efforts require clear understanding of our opponents: their manner, methods, and motives.

About the Author and the Muslim Consultants

My formal education includes an undergraduate degree from the University of California at Berkeley, a master's degree from Princeton

Theological Seminary, and a doctorate from Fuller Theological Seminary. My informal education began when, as a child, I was coached by my mother in scripture memorization and by my father in simple theological awareness. So the foundation for my basic convictions was laid early in scripture, which I began to read as a chapter-a-day commitment at the age of twelve. My faith was nurtured in my home and in our local congregation. In the Gospels, I saw Jesus repeatedly reach out beyond the accepted circle of religious institutionalism to touch and bless the lives of diverse people who needed his accepting love. He first loved people and met their needs, and then sought to share the truth that motivated his love. As his truth was experienced, it brought transforming power to the lives he touched.

During the two years we talked and worked together, my primary Muslim consultant, Dr. Shalahudin Kafrawi, was the professor of philosophy and religion at Moravian College in Bethlehem, Pennsylvania. He is now the professor of philosophy and Islamic studies at Hobart and William Smith College in Geneva, New York. He is a Sunni Muslim from Indonesia and is fluent in Arabic and English as well as two languages of Indonesia. He has a master of arts in Islamic studies from McGill University. His PhD in Islamic philosophy and theology is from Binghamton University. Dr. Kafrawi edited much of my early material to be sure it correctly reflects a valid interpretation of Islam. He also wrote the rough draft of the chapter on the Five Pillars of Islam, explained a valid method of interpreting the Qur'an, and briefly reflected on Muslim spirituality.

My second Muslim consultant, Medhat AR Reiser, was born to a Muslim family in Cairo, Egypt. He has a graduate degree in chemical engineering from Cairo University and did additional graduate work at L'Ecole d'Application des Poudres in Paris, France. He is amazingly perceptive at discerning delicate shades of meaning as I explain a spiritual point, and he unerringly gives clarity and focus to my position. He has become a trusted comrade as we share our lives.

These two men have been invaluable in guiding my Islamic awareness. Over the many months of our collaboration we have formed a bond that has included study, reflection, and prayer.

Founding Father John Adams is reputed to have said, "Facts are stubborn things." In our day of fear and confusion, writers often find it difficult to stay with the facts and trust readers to draw their own conclusions. As a Christian-Muslim team, we believe there are objective facts that need to be known. Like Adams, we believe in the value of stubborn facts. We are therefore committed to God and to each other to carefully confine ourselves to facts that can be objectively documented. Accurate research and reporting is emphasized, since much that is said and printed about Islam since 9/11 is conjecture and half-truth. We are working together to bring a bifocal presentation of the multifaceted reality of Islam as a major faith and a review of key facts from Islamic history. Only with this valid information can Jewish, Christian, and Muslim neighbors interact with openness and confidence. Ignorance of the facts negatively influences the highly charged state of the world in which we live. Thus our goal is to offer historical, religious, and biographical content that will encourage all readers to use the screen of their own experience to draw wise conclusions and then participate in building strong community relationships and wise national policy. We believe that truth validates truth. If we openly and lovingly share our own deep spiritual convictions without rancor, the truth we represent will bear its own witness as God wills us to use it.

While respecting the spiritual commitment of the others, each of us as collaborators on this project remains true to our own faith. Nor does our collegial relationship imply that any one of us accepts the other faith positions as equally valid to our own. My faith position is the centrality of Christ and the Gospel as the motivation for my life. Dr. Kafrawi's and Mr. Reiser's faith positions are the centrality of Muhammad and the truth of the Qur'an as the spiritual motivation for their lives. Concerning the source of ultimate spiritual truth, we agree to respectfully disagree, trusting God to ultimately preserve and reveal the truth.

In working together, the three of us have come to agree that our respect for the others' integrity compels us to believe that there is much to be gained, for ourselves and for the faith we hold, by cooperative and supportive dialogue. The full and glorious counsel of God is beyond the complete comprehension of any mortal. I pray that what is expressed here will be useful to you, our readers. If points are made that seem incorrect, please free my two friends from all responsibility. I alone am responsible for what will be included in the final draft.

The Critical Two-Faith Dilemma: A Cause for Hostility or Hope for Collaboration

A significant issue needs to be recognized: both Christianity and Islam present themselves as the ultimate revelation of divine truth. Each believes that God has willed his people to express their particular faith in an effort to win the world. Each believes that God has called them to build creative, Godly communities of virtue and peace. Only through sensitive listening to God and each other can we creatively function amid such a challenge. Our method of communication must model the virtue of our message; if not, the result will be more hostility and bloodshed. Our life witness and our methods of love and integrity are the most significant means to communicate the truth that we share. It is time to be deeply committed to our faith, open to the witness of others, and let God sort out our differences.

Neither radical, belligerent Islam nor militant, self-righteous Christianity is a valid representation of the faith it claims. Each interacting with the other in hostility is quite capable of blowing our earth apart. In response to this frightening possibility, the one bias that we bring to this task is a sincere desire to let almighty God use this effort to build greater understanding. As has been true throughout history, informed people of faith, despite incredible differences, have been inspired to join together in heroic efforts of healing and social renewal. By God's grace, may this renewal happen again in our time.

A Personal Confession and Final Challenge

Throughout my more than fifty years as a pastor, I taught that Jesus is the only way to salvation, that only the Bible teaches the true way to God, and that the scriptures of the Old and New Testament contain all the truth needed for salvation and a holy life pleasing to God. These three foundational beliefs continue to guide me.

In my research for this book, however, I have met Islamic people who bear witness to God's love and truth in a vital way. Their witness as Muslims to the saving grace of God in their daily lives is an inspiration. Thus, some readers may still be puzzled: How can I reconcile my recent experiences of observing the vitality of Muslim faith with my lifelong

Kenneth B. Cragg

commitment to the centrality of Christ? The teaching of Jesus recorded in Matthew 22 is a key to my comfort in this matter.

In response to the Pharisee's question, "What is the greatest commandment?" Jesus replied by quoting from the ancient Jewish scriptures, "You shall love the Lord your God with all your heart, and with all your soul, and with all your mind. This is the greatest and first commandment. And a second is like it: You shall love your neighbor as yourself."

In "A Common Word between Us and You," a 2008 letter written by Muslim scholars to the international Christian community, we hear this same reply by Jesus quoted as their key focus. Here we see a divine truth first articulated in Jewish teaching, then highlighted by Jesus as the focus of divine law. Now in our time, modern Muslim leaders quote this same text to highlight their message of reconciliation to the Christian community. I find in all of this a sign that God is calling all his people to himself through this fundamental truth they hold in common: love for God and love for neighbor.

So, in that spirit, as a committed follower of Christ, I share with you in these pages the stirring story of Muhammad as well as his message, which has been betrayed by the radical terrorist movement. Perhaps the life and message of Muhammad will startle and inspire you, as it has me, to sense God drawing his people together in a new tri-faith bond of love. This bond will herald a day of peace. In a thoughtful reading of this book, you may sense this as a new possibility.

I therefore encourage you to read thoughtfully, with your heart open to what God may be saying. Spiritual revival and healing is possible in our time when faithful Christians and Muslims agree to work together. Perhaps, strangely and wonderfully, Christians and Muslims will become partners for peace.

Acknowledgments

Jane and Greg Cook gave inspiration when mine was in short supply. They provided the knowledge of writing and publishing that I never had. To be clear, this book would have been impossible without their love, wisdom, and sacrificial help.

Many friends and family supported this effort with valuable advice and wise counsel. I especially appreciate the suggestions of my beloved daughters-in-law Kay and Vivian Cragg, who guarded me from overstatement and rash judgment, and son-in-law Jim Teahan, who gave time and attention in the early rigors of editing.

I owe great appreciation to colleagues and friends who reassured me in my efforts and gave valuable suggestions for content along the way. Of special value have been the help from devoted friend Bill Arnold, wise and supportive critic Dr. Clarke Chapman, ministerial colleague the Reverend Steve Shussett, wise neighbor Dr. Robert Wright and, for his inspiration and pastoral love, the Reverend Bill Lentz. Of special significance has been the friendship of Abdulla Bozkurt and Fahrudin Mekic, two Muslim gentlemen who have shared their lives and faith with me over the past several years.

Beyond compare or description has been the love and constant, dedicated support of my dear wife, Willa Cragg.

Introduction

The events of September 11, 2001 posed a defiant threat to world peace, yet most Americans remain unaware of the historical background that gave rise to these crimes against humanity. We responded then, and are reacting even now, to the broader, international radical movement without knowing what motivates the terrorists. It should come as no surprise that we are poorly equipped to fight the battle. A lack of historical understanding stands in the way of our ability to distinguish between those who pervert Islam and those who are followers of true Islam. Specifically, we need clarity on at least six relevant issues:

- Who are the terrorists, and why have they targeted the Western world?
- How does current terrorist activity relate to the historic Muslim faith?
- What is the origin and nature of historic Islam?
- Who was the Prophet Muhammad, and how do his teachings relate to today's world?
- How can the American people respond creatively to issues of security?
- How should American Christians and Jews relate to the American Muslim population?

Christians and Muslims: From History to Healing addresses each of these vitally important questions by exploring Islam's history, the radical terrorist movement, and emerging spiritual responses. Extensive information about the Prophet Muhammad and Islam provides the facts needed to analyze the radical movement and its perverted distortion of true Islam. The book also provides a foundation to help Christian and Jewish faith communities effectively relate to their Muslim neighbors. These informational tools will inform the reader and aid in building a healthy, proactive response to the ongoing international faith crisis.

To fearfully compromise freedom and justice by marginalizing loyal Muslim Americans is not only anti-Muslim, it is also anti-American. The goal of this book is to affirm the core value of the Gospel, "love for God and love for neighbor." As we live this affirmation, we will keep our American values strong while promoting our national security.

A Special Word to Jewish Readers

The author acknowledges a major dependence on historic Judaism for the ethical and social dynamics of Christianity and Islam. Even though this dependence is not emphasized, it is fundamental. The author hopes that the Jewish faith community will undertake the same task of understanding as that outlined for the Christian community, especially as described in Chapter 12.

A Special Word to Evangelical Christian Readers

The author is personally related to this part of the Christian church by birth and tradition. To this spiritual community he owes his passion and holds out his hope that we lovingly embrace Muslims as children of God. We who hold strong theological foundations, however, often write off people who are outside the focus of our spiritual comfort zone, cataloguing them as alien before acknowledging their humanity and engaging in a dialogue with them about their beliefs. While holding fully to what God has revealed to us, may we dare to welcome, accept, and love all whom God puts in our path.

A Special Word to Muslim Readers

While you will quickly sense that this book is written by a Christian and is addressed most especially to that faith community, I encourage you to fully participate in the task of bridge-building with other concerned people of the monotheistic faiths. In my recent years of exploring Islam and being accepted by Muslim people of various national backgrounds, I have become aware that God has given us similar gifts of faith and truth. As we know and respect each other, we are more fully blessed in our own faiths and more effective in our outreach to people who lack the hope and strength of a spiritual understanding.

The Prophet Muhammad was sent by God to share faith and hope with a world in darkness and ignorance. Muhammad referred often to Jews and Christians as People of the Book. As we support and strengthen each other, God's ultimate goal of claiming the people of the world will surely progress more effectively. That is my aim in writing this book—that the divine purpose of God may be honored and fulfilled.

As we embrace the common vision of peace and communal strength taught by Jesus and Muhammad, we surely draw closer to the goal God has for all humanity. Although we see God's goal unfolding in profoundly different ways within each of our faith expressions, the blessings of justice and peace are common benefits that we may all share together.

Thus this book offers the call to all monotheistic people to find in Jesus and Muhammad a powerful alternative to hostility and international disaster.

The truth of the matter is amazing and wonderful: Jesus and Muhammad, although very different, have much in common. Sharing their spiritual quest can deepen and expand our own faith commitment while leading us into a rich and meaningful approach to international peace.

Section I–
Two Faces of Islam

The students in my world religion classes at Northampton Community College in Tannersville, Pennsylvania, represent the wonderfully broad diversity of American culture. These young adults seek honest answers to questions about international terrorism in the context of a society that includes Hindus, Buddhists, Jews, Muslims, and Christians. Their spiritual concerns are often naïve, but urgent. At times, my mind and heart struggle when leading these class discussions. In part, this book is my response.

So in a sense the book is motivated by my love for my students. More accurately, it is about God's love, which gives all of his people the creative power to love in the best and the worst conditions of life. Starting where God often meets us, at the deepest point of our concern, we acknowledge the issue of terrorism, perpetrated by radicals claiming to act in the name of Islam. In setting forth the stark facts about terrorist activity, I wish to be clear: I do so with both a deep sense of concern as well as a deep sense of hope, even confidence. A personal anecdote will explain my reason for confidence.

As a nineteen-year-old infantryman stationed in Germany during World War II, I participated in a surprising exchange of trust with two teenaged German prisoners of war. On two occasions, we talked together in halting English/German about passages from the New

Testament as we bounced along in a convoy truck on the long trek to a forced labor site.

A few days after the second conversation, an accident occurred. As I attempted to jump down from the bed of the truck after the prisoners were unloaded, my left boot was tangled in the tailgate rope. The truck moved forward, and the rope pulled free, but not before violently yanking me off my feet and sending my rifle and me flying in different directions. At that moment, only the two youthful prisoners with whom I had been speaking saw what had occurred and realized that I was injured.

Without considering the risk they took as prisoners under guard, one rushed to help me while the other retrieved my rifle and quickly put it in my hands. All this was done before the other guards realized what had happened. Only weeks before, we had been armed enemies faced off in battle, but the power of a new spiritual bond turned enemies into committed friends.

God's love expressed by human beings in the midst of pain and destruction often defies human understanding. Over and over, the power of love has been made clear to me in a maze of unexpected ways and places. It is my faith in the power of God's love to change and refashion life that assures me that if we obey the call of God, his love will prevail.

Chapter 1

The Peril of Radical Terror

In *New Seeds of Contemplation*, Thomas Merton wrote this about faith: "True faith is never merely a source of spiritual doubt. It may indeed bring peace, but before it does so, it must involve us in struggle. A 'faith' that avoids this struggle is really a temptation against true faith."[1]

The struggle of faith is especially pointed in Islam today as Muslims examine how they will respond creatively to what many perceive to be the godless secularism and modernity in the Western world. The radical terrorist activity that has emerged in the past fifty years is a tragically destructive aspect of this reformation process.

The Arabic word *jihad* means to endeavor or struggle. Muslims manifest jihad in two ways: as an inner effort to achieve spiritual purity or as a political means of safeguarding the *umma* or community. Faithful Muslims struggle to maintain spiritual consistency and purity across the globe in the twenty-first century. Radical Muslims take advantage of this tension by emphasizing political action solely. To the world's peril, the terrorist activity that has emerged in the past fifty years distorts the true meaning of jihad.

Faithfulness is not limited to an inner commitment. It is keyed to outward action. Part of the struggle of all faithful people is to build bridges of understanding. An Arabic proverb says, in essence, "Those who would build bridges must be willing to be walked on." Though our perceptions are diverse, even contradictory, and our understanding is uncertain, may God grant each of us the courage to be personally involved. When we are faithful, the truth may win some surprising battles. We might very well join unexpected friends to win this struggle against our common enemies of radical terrorism and anarchy.

Some Specifics of Recent Terror Activity

I give credit to my father for humorous wisdom, obvious here in his reflection on the great flood: "The only reason Noah could stand the stench inside the Ark was because he was fully aware of the storm outside."

First we look at the storm: the terror that appears to threaten the social stability of our planet. Then we will explore the ark of faith that offers peace, justice, and social stability. Understandably, the public focus on recent terror turns to the horror of September 11, 2001, but unfortunately, the issues of terrorism and its tragic consequences are far greater than that pivotal tragedy. Reflection on this partial list of devastating terror attacks may help clarify the critical importance of our struggle.[2]

Date	Event	Deaths	Attributed to
Jan. 1972	Olympic Games, Munich Germany	11	PLO
Sep. 1974	TWA explosion, Ionian Sea	88	Unknown
Apr. 1983	US Embassy, Beirut, Lebanon	63	Hezbollah
Oct. 1983	US Marine barracks, Lebanon	241	Hezbollah
Dec. 1988	Pan Am explosion, Scotland	140	Libya
Feb. 1993	NY World Trade Center bomb	7	al Qaeda
Aug. 1998	US Embassies, Kenya and Tanzania	302	al Qaeda
Oct. 2000	USS *Cole*, Yemen	16	al Qaeda
Sept. 2001	NY World Trade Center; Pentagon; PA	3000	al Qaeda
Dec. 2001	Foiled American Airlines shoe bomb	0	al Qaeda
May 2010	Foiled NY Times Square SUV bomb	0	Taliban

Beyond these notable terrorist actions are thousands of documented instances of terror exacted against individuals, political structures, and social groups in the last forty years worldwide. Most of this terrorist activity has been carried out against moderate Muslims living within

4

nations that oppose radical Islam. For example, during 2007 and 2008, terrorist infiltration became the dominant concern for Pakistan. Taliban insurgents moved in from the mountain border between Pakistan and Afghanistan, and radicals pushing east from Iraq set up camps. The governments of these countries have often been incapable of making an adequate response. For these and other reasons, it is impossible to make a clear separation between moderate and radical Islam, by nation or by group.

These continuing events keep the tension constant and tempt us to irrationally project our hostility onto our own loyal Muslim citizens, a fault that we must help each other avoid. Rather, we must direct our energy to fully understand the background and motivation behind the terror menace and work together as an interfaith people to make our communities stronger.

Exploring this broad picture thoughtfully, we find four patterns of organized terror. It is of value to thoughtfully note their subtle differences.

1. The first pattern is found in fairly stable, moderate Muslim countries. Radical cells implement unrest and try to force the terrorist agenda into the mainstream government and culture. We see this happening, for example, in Indonesia and Pakistan.

2. The second pattern appears in countries already roiled by injustices. In these places, radical forces can more easily stir up emotion and criminal action against the local authorities. This is expressed in random attacks, such as those seen in Israel, intended to focus attention on the displacement of the Palestinians. The radical action is politically motivated to influence local policy as well as world opinion.

3. We see a slightly different pattern of localized terror within European nations, where terror cells are made up of radicalized immigrant youths who perceive themselves to be excluded from equal participation in their adopted homeland. Some of these youths have received training in local *madrassas*, private Muslim academies, located in Spain, the Netherlands, Germany, France, England, and, recently, the United States. Often these academies are funded by

Middle Eastern oil money and presided over by instructors sent by the funding institution.

4. Finally, there is the grand, overarching disdain for the West and for what is referred to in various ways as its corruption, immorality, and hubris. Terrorist networks capitalize on this attitude, which is particularly expressed and promoted by al Qaeda. In a video delivered to Al Jazeera television network offices in Kabul, Afghanistan in early October 2001, Osama bin Laden boldly declared:

> I have only a few words for America and its people: I swear by God Almighty who raised the heavens without effort that neither America nor anyone who lives there will enjoy safety until safety becomes a reality for us living in Palestine and before all the infidel armies leave the land of Muhammad.[3]

This al Qaeda commitment has been played out in a broad series of attacks, the most notable, of course, being the trauma of 9/11.

Subtle Emotional and Social Threats

In addition to the physical danger involved in the ongoing terror threat, we need to face other equally significant psychological and social challenges and discover appropriate responses. Two social issues became especially challenging in 2010. One was the backlash to the TV comedy show *South Park* that appeared to mock the Prophet Muhammad. Members of the *South Park* production team were threatened, and one show in late April 2010 was reportedly censored in response to the threat.

The other far more inflammatory issue was the proposed building of a Muslim community center and mosque two blocks from Ground Zero in lower Manhattan. This debate, initially a local New York City concern, blossomed into a national spectacle not yet resolved as this book goes to print. Politicians and stress mongers of all stripes have stirred hatred toward Muslims by capitalizing on the sensitivities of some who lost loved ones in the 9/11 catastrophe at the World Trade Center. In so doing, they have played into the hands of radical terrorists, who are all too eager for proof that the United States is fundamentally anti-Muslim. Thus our concern is not only what our enemies can do to us physically, but also what they can do to us emotionally and morally as we face our own pain and insecurity.

As one commentator pointed out, in our nation we do not confuse Boston Roman Catholics with the Irish Republican Army bomb squad. Yet we confuse people wanting a Muslim community center in lower Manhattan with the radical Muslim terrorists of the Middle East. We must learn to make these distinctions, or we are in danger of losing the support of the millions of peace-loving Muslims who still champion our cause around the globe. Osama bin Laden did us grave damage, but if we betray our own people in misguided fear, he will have won a major international victory. It will take maturity and courage to hold high the torch of freedom to all law-abiding citizens in our midst while candidly acknowledging the radical terrorists who seek our national destruction. Or will we surrender to fear and confusion as we did in 1942, when we hustled thousands of our loyal Japanese citizens off to relocation camps in the arid wastes of Utah and Nevada?

We can no longer rest confident in our ignorance and see Islam either as one great dangerous monolith or as simply a peaceful religion embarrassed by radicals. Islam is a vast, convoluted collection of divergent groups with observable loyalties and discernable patterns. With careful study, we can gain fuller awareness and learn to embrace our friends and isolate our enemies.

The Danger of Cultural Adaptation

Another threat is naively responding to a Muslim social complaint by changing the law. In some circles, this approach to resolving Muslim social concerns is known as stealth jihad, the process of slowly invading a culture and gaining social consensus to implement Shari'ah law. This is a subtle yet effective strategy to transform a culture without a violent overthrow, one that Muslims, or any immigrant other group, can slowly accomplish from within.

Such a danger may seem innocuous on the surface. Here's a recent example. In May of 2006, cab drivers of Somali Muslim descent began to refuse fares at the Minneapolis St. Paul International Airport on religious grounds. They objected to participating in the commercial transport of alcohol.

Airport protocol calls for drivers who refuse a fare to return to the end of the cab line. But claiming religious stigma was involved, the Somali drivers appealed to the Metropolitan Airports Commission (MAC) for authorization to refuse service to a potential customer on religious grounds without being sent to the back of the airport waiting line.

MAC contacted the Minnesota chapter of the Muslim American Society (MAS) for help in mediating the dispute. Together, they considered whether to install color-coded lights atop the Somali non-alcohol cabs to officially distinguish them from other cabs. Then taxi starters at the airport would know where to direct passengers carrying wine or liquor.

In the midst of this dispute, Katherine Kersten, staff writer at the *Minneapolis StarTribune,* quoted a nationally recognized expert on Somali society at Macalester College, Ahmed Samatar: "There is a general Islamic prohibition against drinking, but carrying alcohol for people in commercial enterprise has never been forbidden. There is no basis in Somali cultural practice or legal tradition for that."[4]

Then why did the Somali drivers raise the issue in the first place? The answer, as reported in the *StarTribune,* is that the Muslim American Society had issued a *fatwa* (religious edict). "The fatwa proclaims that 'Islamic jurisprudence' prohibits taxi drivers from carrying passengers with alcohol, 'because it involves cooperating in sin according to Islam.'"[5]

At the very least, this situation reveals a conflict of interest for the Muslim American Society, which, by issuing a fatwa, appeared to be causing dissension, not seeking solutions. Furthermore, the MAS has roots in the Middle East, not Africa (where Somalia is located), giving credence to the idea that it was using the Somali drivers to advance its own cause, not one based on Somali cultural practice.

Even if the MAS interpretation of Shari'ah law had been accurate, theirs is the type of action that, over time, could instill aspects of Muslim Shari'ah law in American governing and regulatory bodies, thereby changing the social and legal structure of a community.

Additional confusion arises in the discussion of Shari'ah law when no distinction is made between its applications in general social policy, such as was initially intended in the cab driver dispute, versus its limited use in the regulation of Muslim religious obligations, such as the daily prayer ritual and giving to the poor. The faith-based application of Shari'ah is a protected religious right in American society, while the former could be seen as a potential invasion of American culture.

After much deliberation, The Metropolitan Airport Commissions in Minneapolis refused the drivers' petition and did not agree to install special lights on Muslim cabs. If the MAC had conducted a less-than-careful investigation, they could have been tricked into being the first public agency in the United States to impose a regulation based on Shari'ah law and enforced on US property. In compassionately responding to our Muslim countrymen, unless caution is observed, we could unintentionally give aid and support to the underlying goals of our enemy. It is of note that another American Muslim organization, Islamic Pluralism, appears to have served as a whistleblower in wisely guiding the decision in Minneapolis. It is important for us to know who our friends are.

The overall question remains: How do we achieve a balance of compassionate support for legitimate Muslim religious practice and social concerns while consistently maintaining our constitutional safeguards of freedom and justice?

In a *Wall Street Journal* article entitled "Making Muslim Integration Work," former British Prime Minister Tony Blair offered his perspective:[6]

> Most people instinctively understand the right approach to integration. We just have to articulate and enforce it. This approach is to distinguish clearly and carefully between the common space, shared by all citizens, and the space where we can be different. We have different faiths. We practice them differently. We have different histories, different cultures and different views….But there has to be a shared acceptance that some things we believe in and we do together: obedience to certain

values like democracy, rule of law, equality between men and women; respect for national institutions; and speaking the national language. This common space cannot be left to chance or individual decision. It has to be accepted as mandatory. Doing so establishes a clear barrier between those citizens of the host community who are concerned for understandable reasons and those who are bigoted.

How Do We Respond?

Muslim people, the second largest religious group in the world, are loyal to the original goals of the Prophet Muhammad, who promoted social stability, moral purity, spiritual devotion to God, and peace. They are people who seek to build their lives, love their families, and express their devotion to God without fear and in peace, just as most of us do.[7]

Many people have no clue how to distinguish a highly respectable Muslim citizen from a dangerous individual supporting radical terrorist beliefs. The content of this book is directed at finding a solution to this problem. We must not continue to live in the state of ignorant naïveté that was this author's state before 9/11. The threat we face is very real, and only concerned, knowledgeable citizens are in a position to cooperatively safeguard our principles and our lives.

As we make this study, we need to be aware of the varied faces of Islam. We need a keen awareness of the critical danger that radical terrorism holds for our world while keeping in mind that vast numbers of God-fearing Muslims are themselves often the first targets of the radicals.

Despite all that has been documented on the continuing activity of the terrorist movement, some of us in the United States are living in denial. Since we have not felt the danger directly in recent years, we choose to ignore it. In contrast, others acknowledge the issue with emotional and verbal intensity. Many in this latter group sincerely believe that militant counter-terror is the only proper response. It is important that we recognize that neither of these extremes is valid or wise. This will become clear as we explore the broader issues and then consider a series of proactive approaches to counter radical terrorist activity with the spirit and power of our faith.

Many books on Islam and on the terrorist movement have recently been published. This book will clarify the issues and offer a strong moral alternative. Our first loyalty is to God. This loyalty is more urgent than our concern for our national or personal safety. Paradoxically, it is in the midst of answering God's call to love our neighbor as ourselves that we find the true source of security. I urge you to read this book prayerfully and carefully consider the spirit-oriented proposals it offers.

Reflection

Since 9/11, America has sought to come to grips with the various challenges related to terror and other radical, disruptive influences from abroad. This has been greatly complicated by the religious content apparently motivating our enemy. The terror groups claim that Islam is their motivation. Yet recognized Muslim leaders from around the world repudiate the tactics of terror and claim the terrorists are hijacking their religion.

Herein lies the challenge as we seek to defend ourselves and our way of life. Who is the enemy? What are the ramifications of the radical assault? How are we to respond? The answers to these questions are available to any responsible citizen. Look to this book as a beginning point. We need not succumb to ignorant provocations aimed at portraying Muslims as evil, nor do we need to take foolish risks in supporting a potential enemy.

Are we well enough informed? Are we truly open to deeper understanding? And, most important, are we willing to honestly lay aside our preconceptions and seek the will of God in the struggle? Knowledge, love, and wisdom must be our guide.

Chapter 2

A Summary of the Islamic Faith

Having reviewed the horror of terrorist destruction, we now examine the true face of Islam, a sharp contrast. The common heritage shared by Judaism, Christianity, and Islam serves as our starting point, followed by consideration of the three basic concepts that make up the Islamic belief system. Noting the many similarities and differences among the three monotheistic faiths can help clarify the difficult issues facing today's world.

The Tri-Faith Bridge

As most Jews and Christians well understand, their faith traditions are traced through Abraham, Isaac, and Jacob. In Genesis 17:5, God declared that he had made Abraham the father of many nations. Indeed, Abraham's son Isaac fathered Jacob, whose twelve sons are the ancestors of the twelve tribes of Israel, the origin of the Jewish community. One of Jacob's sons, Judah, is the ancestor of Mary[1], leading us to Jesus and Christianity.

Hebrew scripture makes it clear that Islam also shares this common heritage. Abraham's first son Ishmael had twelve sons, among them Kedar, from whom Muhammad is directly descended. This lineage from Abraham establishes the tri-faith bridge that unites the three great monotheistic faiths.

The tri-faith bridge also takes us into the ethical foundation of the three monotheistic faiths. As described in Exodus 20, God gave the Ten Commandments to Moses, yet Christians, Muslims, and Jews all acknowledge them as their essential standard of moral conduct. (It is interesting to note that Moses is mentioned in the Qur'an more often than any other prophetic leader except Muhammad.) Through the commandments, each faith tradition finds God's moral direction in the affairs of government, community, and personal morality.

The commonalities don't end with the Ten Commandments. Islam honors the Torah, the Psalms, and the Gospels while focusing on the revelation of the Qur'an made known to Muhammad by the angel Gabriel. The Qur'an also refers to many of the patriarchal and prophetic voices of Judaism, such as Adam, Noah, Abraham, Moses, among others. Finally, the Qur'an mentions notable people of the Gospels, including John the Baptist, the Virgin Mother Mary and her son Jesus, the Messiah. Whereas Christianity in the New Testament gives the apostle Paul a major role, six hundred years later the Qur'an honors all the people listed above except Paul and gives the primary place to the Prophet Muhammad.

A difference in perspective between the Christian and Muslim faiths emerges in the account of the testing of Abraham, which is found in both the Bible and the Qur'an. Although both stories have God commanding Abraham to sacrifice his son, the crucial difference is that in Genesis 22:1–19, Isaac does not know that he is the sacrifice until his father actually binds him in preparation and lays him on the altar. In Surah 37:100–110, Abraham's son Ishmael is to be the sacrifice. Ishmael knows this beforehand and prays that he will be worthy. In both stories, of course, God declares Abraham worthy for his total obedience and spares the son.

Christians understand this story as a foreshadowing of the suffering of Jesus and atonement for human sin. Thus it is God's grace that takes center stage for Christians. Muslims, however, emphasize total submission by father and son, highlighting the importance of human surrender and obedience to God. For Muslims, it is not possible for anyone to suffer in their stead as a means of atonement. In fact, trying to do so would be an immoral act.

Both the Bible and the Qur'an contain the common ethical standard of love for God and love for neighbor. In the Christian revelation, the power that inspires this love is the redemptive healing grace of God, declared in the passion and resurrection of Jesus. For Muslims, this love is achieved through submission to God, the alpha and omega of Islamic teaching.

Basic Islamic Beliefs

The Islamic belief system can most easily be divided into three concepts, which are spelled out in the Qur'an, the Hadith, and the Shari'ah:

1. Islam requires faith in God and all that God teaches.
2. The five pillars of Islam form the ritual foundation for Muslim life.
3. Muslims are held to high ethical standards, which ultimately will determine their eternal destination.

Faith in God and all that God teaches. In its simplest expression, the primary faith of Islam is the centrality of God as the one and only Creator who sustains all of life and is the source of guidance for all people. Recognizing this fundamental truth results in a unified view of existence. It rejects any sense of divisions or partnership in the divine reality. God, the essence of the divine being, is the sole source of all power and authority and is therefore entitled to be worshipped and obeyed by all humankind.

The focus of Islamic devotion to God is perhaps best expressed in contemporary English by the term *obedience*. The honor, respect, and love a Muslim has for God are demonstrated by submission of the human will, or *surrender*. In fact, *surrender* is the correct translation of the Arabic word *Islam*.

As a Muslim kneels in prayer, prostrating his body with forehead to the earth or floor, he is expressing love for God in full submission and in the deepest respect for the divine being, the one and only God. This sense of surrender is demonstrated not only through the daily rituals of Islam but also through each activity of life. The devout Jew, Christian, and Muslim appear to express their devotion to God in vastly different ways; however, when carefully examined, the inner devotion is much the same. They would each agree that all of life is intended to be a loving response to God—for all three faiths, the primary issues are willing obedience, devout prayerful worship, and a correct understanding of divine truth.

In Islam, the reality and truth of God are revealed to humanity in two significant ways. The first means of revelation is through prophets, the messengers who from the time of Adam have spoken on behalf of God. They each urged the people of their time to obey and worship God alone and none other. Whenever the prophetic teachings were distorted or ignored, God sent another prophet to bring humanity back to the straight path.

Beginning with Adam, the chain of prophets includes Noah, Abraham, Ishmael, Isaac, Lot, Jacob, Joseph, Moses, preeminently Jesus, and ultimately Muhammad. Each of these prophets is acknowledged as a holy messenger, and when each name is written, the phrase "peace be upon him" (or pbuh, for short) follows the mention of the name. In time, some of God's revelations to these prophets were codified in sacred texts known to us as the Torah, Psalms, the Gospel, and the Qur'an.

The Qur'an is an amazing collection of spiritual, ethical, and policy statements directed to Muhammad by the angel Gabriel. According to language specialists, the Arabic in the Qur'an sets the standard for classical language perfection. Since Muhammad could neither read nor write, the quality of Arabic found in the Qur'an has caused Muslim scholars to consider that it was revealed to Muhammad in a miraculous way. The first revelation came unexpectedly on the "Night of Power" in 610 CE in a cave on Mount Hira, when the angel Gabriel confronted Muhammad. He claimed the Qur'an and its revelations to be the only miracle of his life. The revelations continued until his death in 632 CE.

Muhammad received the early revelations in Mecca, and they contain the initial spiritual guidance of the Islamic faith. The content is similar to material found in Exodus, with specific teachings on moral practice and worship. The later revelations were primarily given in Medina while the Prophet was guiding the new community in matters of the faith as well as defending it from attack by the Meccan army. This later content resembles material in Leviticus and Joshua as it gives directions on everything from settling quarrels to waging defensive battle. Both parts, like much of the Bible, are more valuable when read in the context of what was occurring when the text was given; thus, whether revealed in Mecca or Medina, the location is noted above each chapter, or Surah.

The Qur'an was organized into a single, written Arabic volume some years after the Prophet's death. A curious design was chosen for its organization. There is a short introductory chapter. Then all the material is set forth in terms of each chapter's length, regardless of content or place of origin. Surah 2 is the longest and Surah 114 is the shortest. When exploring a specific subject of the faith, the use of the concordance commonly located at the end of the Qur'an is an essential aid.

As language students recognize, poetry cannot be translated in all its nuances. Since the Qur'an was revealed in classical Arabic poetry, the full sense of its message is best communicated in its original Arabic form. For this reason, Muslim parents living in Western countries desire their children to learn Arabic.

Surah 8:29 briefly declares the focus of the Qur'an:

> O you who believe! If you keep your duty to
> Allah, He will give you discrimination [between
> right and wrong] and will rid you of your evil
> thoughts and deeds, and will forgive you. Allah
> is of infinite bounty.

Walter H. Wagner, a scholarly student of the Qur'an, offers helpful insight into an overarching awareness of the Qur'anic message:

> The Qur'an contains the principles and often
> specifics regarding family relations, inheritance,
> divorce, sexual conduct, speech and dress, and
> personal privacy, along with stipulations about
> war, treatment of captives and slaves, and
> punishment of criminals. These are interwoven
> with exhortations to prayer, care for the poor,
> acknowledging God's sovereignty, and the divine
> plan for the cosmos. God calls on the believers
> to study the Qur'an for knowledge of the nature
> of the world, history, and the proper functioning
> of a God-ruled society, and through that study

> to come to know and be obedient to the God in Whom is genuine freedom ... The Qur'an frames and then gives the content, structure, and standards for living the Islamic life for individuals, the whole Muslim community (umma), and relations to other people under the gracious and just rule of God.[2]

As we engage the Qur'an, it is vital that we recognize that the unique nature of the monotheistic faith, based on the call of Abraham, is consistently revealed in the context of historical circumstance. Even statements appearing to lack all connection to a narrative are nevertheless heavily dependent on the place and time of the revelation. Gaining the full sense of the statements of Jesus offers a vivid illustration of this point. In the Sermon on the Mount, Jesus says, "And if anyone forces you to go one mile, go also the second mile" (Matthew 5:41).

On the surface, the text appears only to encourage feelings of helpful generosity. However, on looking closely at the context, quite a different meaning subtly emerges. The key word is *forces*. Jesus spoke this teaching when the Roman government occupied Judea. Under their rule, any Jew could be conscripted on a moment's notice to carry a Roman soldier's pack for a mile. In the midst of stressful conditions, Jesus was counseling us to carry the pack a second mile, to respond to hostile or unreasonable demands with courteous and generous compliance, overwhelming our offenders with a sense of grace.

An awareness of the context is critical to grasping the point of Jesus. In the same way, the interpretation of the Qur'an must always take into consideration the specific context under which it was inspired. Muhammad frequently appears to receive divine guidance in the midst of social problems as he is building a new society in Medina. Many of the Qur'anic statements are highly dependent for their meaning on the specific circumstance at the time.

Taken out of context, a passage of the Qur'an (Surah 9:5) has caused much confusion. This is the first Qur'anic verse mentioned in the *fatwa* of Osama bin Laden following the 9/11 attacks. Bin Laden used this verse to validate these atrocities. It is also a verse that was referred to by the Reverend Franklin Graham[3] in his *60 Minutes* interview on September 30, 2001, when he described Islam as a wicked religion.

Verse 9:5 says:

> When the sacred months are over, slay the
> polytheists (*mushrikun*) wherever you find them,
> and take them [captive] and besiege them, and
> lie in ambush for them everywhere. But if they
> repent and establish the Prayer and pay the
> Zakat, let them go their way. Allah is Forgiving
> and Merciful.

The last sentence of the verse was not included in the quotation by
either bin Laden or Graham.

Contrary to what may be thought from a literal reading of this
translation, this verse is not a *carte blanche* approval to attack any and
all non-Muslim peoples. Here again the issue of historical context is
crucial for our understanding. Verse 9:5 describes the Muslims fighting
the idolaters of Mecca after they had been driven from their homes,
denied their livelihood, and forced to flee for their lives. A commentary
on verse 9:5 from the Islamic Research Institute reads:

> Verse 9:5 was revealed specifically in relation to
> the Muslims fighting the idolaters of Makkah
> (Mecca). The Makkan idolaters are referred to in
> the Qur'an by the technical term "*mushrikun*"
> (sing. "*mushrik*"). This term comes from a three
> letter Arabic root "sh-r-k" which means "to
> associate" or "take a partner unto something,"
> so that the word *mushrikun* literally means,
> "those who take a partner [unto God]," that
> is to say, "polytheists" or "idolaters." It should
> be noted, therefore, that the injunction in this
> verse to fight against the "polytheists" does not
> pertain to either Jews or Christians from the
> point of view of Islamic Law. Interestingly, Jews
> and Christians are never referred to within the
> Qur'an by the term *mushrikun*. They have, in
> fact, a very different "status" or "title" according
> to the Qur'an which, when not addressing them
> as individual communities, often refers to the

two groups together by the technical term, *ahl al-kitab* or "People of the Book," meaning people who have been given a book or scripture by God *other than the Muslims*. Given these facts, it is interesting that this verse should be cited by Bin Laden in the context of a declaration calling on Muslims to fight Jews and Christians, particularly since this verse says nothing about Jews, Christians, or the People of the Book in general.[4]

This careful analysis illustrates the danger of scriptural misinterpretation, which can easily lead to misunderstanding about the actual teachings of Islam. By distorting the message of the Qur'an, Bin Laden leads his followers down a destructive path. We must be on guard against anyone—Christian, Jew, or Muslim—who attempts to manipulate others by misinterpreting holy texts.

Islam teaches life after death, and this profound conviction plays a major role in its influence on the believer. All persons are freely accountable to God and will be judged according to the way they have lived their individual lives. This strong conviction of total individual accountability has been given as a reason why Islam, on moral ground, rejects the Christian doctrine of the atonement. A person who has obeyed and worshipped God will be rewarded with a permanent place of happiness in paradise, usually referred to in the Qur'an as the garden. Those who do not obey and faithfully worship will also receive their just reward—hell, a place of punishment and suffering. Each will receive the justice due for the life they have lived. In many verses, the Qur'an makes these choices vividly clear. Opportunities are also offered to those who recognize the folly of their lives to receive forgiveness and seriously work out a plan of restitution.

Christianity and Islam appear to differ significantly in the matter of community and government regulation. For Islam, all the issues of life directly relate to the wisdom and love of God. Since God is all-knowing and ever-present, the issue of political power would logically be ordered under direct divine guidance. This poses a major challenge as Islam interacts with the world. Walter Wagner says it well:

> The Qur'an and therefore Islam know no
> separation between sacred and secular, material
> and spiritual, reason and revelation, politics and
> worship. The Qur'an gives directions, at times
> commands, to believers and, if they will but
> heed it, to potential believers as well.... All of
> life stems from the Muslim relationship with
> God. Life is of a single essence, the human
> divine relationship.[5]

The ultimate political agenda of Islamic community, or the umma, has always been seen as a common bond embracing spiritual commitment, social structure, and political power. Since God is the Lord of all life, it is only logical that revealed divine truth should determine communal structures and the laws and regulations governing society. This is very much the same logic that was the premise of Christian social structure under the concept of the divine right of kings.

The Qur'an, scripture sent down from God, and the *Hadith*, the way of acting revealed in the words and actions of the Prophet Muhammad, together comprise *Shari'ah* law. Also called *the way*, Shari'ah law provides full guidance for worship, communal structure, and personal morality. Over several centuries, this proved effective in some areas of Islamic society. It was originally administered under the interpretive guidance of a trained body of jurists. The ancient role of the jurists was to continually apply Shari'ah law in the light of the original context in which it was revealed and as it related to the local situations at hand. Thus justice was not arbitrary, but it was administered according to the interrelationship of Islamic universal vision of justice as it related to the local circumstances. This was done in a way similar to the way the Supreme Court of the United States works in interpreting and applying the Constitution. The perceived breakdown of this judicial practice originally led to the emergence of radical extremists seeking to restore Islam to its ancient purity.

The five pillars of Islam form the foundation for Muslim life. Five primary ritual practices of Islam provide Muslims with moral guidance and, above all, an unceasing reminder of the centrality of God in every aspect of human life. Much as the sacraments are external spiritual expressions of Christian faith, so the Pillars of Islam give external expression to a Muslim's commitment to God.

1. ***Shahadah***—A Muslim first needs to believe the truth and then give verbal testimony in the company of others. This verbal testimony consists of two brief articles: "I testify that there is no god but Allah (even in English translation, a Muslim text refers to God using the Arabic term, Allah), and I testify that Muhammad is his messenger." Declaring that testimony in front of other Muslims is the way a new convert enters the faith. To be a good Muslim, one not only follows the truth, but also reaffirms it and gives testimony to it on a daily basis in the five periods of prayer.

2. ***Salat***—The compulsory prayers comprise a specific ritual of words and motions, each somewhat different, as they are offered at five specific times during the waking hours of the day, beginning at dawn and ending with the final prayer prior to retirement. The five prayers are a practical demonstration of faith, and they keep a believer in constant touch with their Creator. Of all the expressions of Islam, the daily prayer is considered the most critical. The five daily prayers develop in a believer the qualities of self-discipline, steadfastness, and obedience to God. The prayers also confirm the call to a daily life of patience, honesty, and truthfulness. Thus flow the five prayers: the first prayer at sunrise, the second at midday, the third in mid-afternoon, the fourth right after sunset, and the fifth at night before retiring. Before starting the prayer, a Muslim needs to be cleansed, as purity is symbolic of coming into the presence of God. The prayer is offered facing Mecca, where the holy shrine, the Ka'ba, is located. Each prayer is initiated by pronouncing *Allahu Akbar* (God is the Greatest).

Friday is the day separated in Islam as the day of worship. The midday ritual prayer is said at the mosque in unison, with men in one area and women in another. The congregation moves through the prayer in a union of word and the ritual movements of standing, kneeling, bowing, and prostrating. Due to a prophetic tradition that suggests a greater benefit comes when prayer is conducted in a group—a benefit twenty-seven times greater than a prayer observed alone—many Muslims prefer to go to the mosque for at least one of the daily prayers. Under special circumstances, such as travel, illness, or other emergencies, arrangements are made so that two prayers may be combined together, with the movements of the prayers shortened. In the case of illness, the prayers are said in a way that doesn't impede the health of the believer. All factors of the five daily prayers lead to the recognition that the constant remembrance of God is the duty of every believer. Through that remembrance, the believer is led to virtue and spiritual consistency. There is no excuse for a Muslim not to observe daily prayer.

3. **Ramadan**—Fasting is the focus of Ramadan, the ninth month of the Islamic lunar calendar. It celebrates the beginning of the Qur'an revelation to Muhammad and is a special time to develop spiritual devotion and self-discipline. The days of Ramadan begin with a predawn meal. After the sun rises and until the sun sets, no food or beverage is consumed, and no sexual activity is engaged in. This self-restraint is practiced for the entire month, the only exception being during pregnancy or periods of ill health. It includes all Muslim people from the time of puberty until old age, when such restrictions might be physically harmful. The Ramadan fast is described in the Qur'an as follows:

> O you who believe! Fasting is prescribed for you, as it was prescribed for those who came before you; that you will perhaps guard yourselves [against evil] ... The month of Ramadan in which the Qur'an was revealed, a guidance for mankind, [a book of] clear proofs of guidance and the criterion [distinguishing between right and wrong]. Therefore whoever of you who is present in that month let him fast (Surah 2:183, 185).

Fasting is both a spiritual training period for the individual, helping to cultivate discipline and spiritual purity, as well as a time to develop empathy for the poor and those who frequently go without. Fasting encourages humility and a sense of closeness to God.

In the evening after sundown, just before or after evening prayer, a meal is held, concluding the day of fasting. This meal is sometimes shared with friends and neighbors in a common bond of spiritual growth as well as a time of relaxed fellowship. Families may also take food to the mosque and share a common meal. After the meal, in the course of the evenings of Ramadan, a person who has memorized the Qur'an reads it aloud in its entirety. Often a special *zakat* (sharing) is given to celebrate God's generosity and to show a special concern for the poor. At the end of Ramadan, the celebration includes a thanksgiving worship at the mosque, a special gift for the poor, and a great, communal feast known as *Id al-Fitr* (breaking the fast). This is the most joyous of the Muslim holidays and a celebration of faith and victory. Ramadan often brings an uplifting sense of joy and renewed energy, along with anticipation that worshippers can face the rest of the year with faithful determination.

4. **Zakat**—The Arabic name of this pillar has no accurate English equivalent, but the basic meaning of the word is to *grow* or *increase*, as well as to be *pure*. The purpose of zakat is to teach generosity in the believer and provide the necessities of life to the poor. As believers share their wealth, its value grows and contributes both to the one who has shared, granting inner purity, and also to the one who has received. In Judaism and Christianity, the expectation is to contribute a tithe, or ten percent of one's income, to the purposes of God. The requirement of zakat in Islam is considerably more. The expected gift is an annual contribution of two and a half percent of a Muslim family's total assets. This money is distributed among the poor and thus serves as a public welfare system in Islamic countries. Giving is seen as an aspect of worship, acknowledging that God is the provider of all. Sharing God's provisions with the poor encourages a sense of communal solidarity and advances the virtue of generosity.

5. **The *Hajj***—An annual pilgrimage (Hajj) to Mecca is the ultimate dramatic expression of the Islamic faith. It is required at least once in the lifetime of each Muslim capable of making the trip and brings together hundreds of thousands of followers from around the world. The Qur'an declares:

> And [remember] when We appointed for Abraham the site of the House, [We said to him]: "Do not associate with Me anything, and purify My House for those who circumambulate [the Ka'ba] and those who stand, and those who bow and prostrate." And proclaim among the people the pilgrimage! They will come to you, on foot and on lean camels, coming from every deep ravine. [They will come] so that they may witness benefits for them, and during the known appointed days they mention the name of Allah, over the beasts of cattle He has provided them. Then eat thereof, and feed the unfortunate and distressed poor (Surah 22:26–28).

This passage of the Qur'an describes the high moment of sacrifice that climaxes the annual hajj celebration at the Ka'ba in Mecca. This annual pilgrimage to Mecca constitutes Islam's most spectacular ritual requirement. It is a memorial of Muhammad's migration from Mecca to Medina when he was about to be killed in a planned ambush, and it is the point when the Islamic calendar begins.

Throughout the few days of the hajj, the pilgrims are reminded frequently of their identity with Abraham. They walk seven times between the two hills in Mecca in memory of Hagar's search for water for her son Ishmael, because the water she found is reputed to have been from the well of Zamzam, near Mecca. The pilgrims throw stones at a pillar in the valley of Nina to commemorate Abraham's rejection of temptation.

Then on the tenth day of the month of Dhu al-hajj, two months and ten days after the end of Ramadan, the pilgrims sacrifice an animal in memory of Abraham's willingness to sacrifice his son in obedience to God's command, as referred to earlier in Surah 37:100–110. This memorial sacrifice is seen as a celebration of faithfulness, not as an act of contrition or redemption of sin, although in some cultures, local Muslim groups have misinterpreted its meaning in this way.

In recent years, as many as two million pilgrims have gathered at one time for the hajj celebration. Together surrounding the Ka'ba, they unite their voices in the same prayer uttered by Muhammad and the early Muslims as they first returned in victory from Medina. Regardless of language, race, ethnicity, national origin, or economic condition, it is here the egalitarian principle is seen most fully as all pilgrims, dressed in identical, simple, white attire symbolizing their solidarity, pray as one the ancient cry of devotion, "*Labbaika Allah-umma, labbaik* (O God, here I am, at your service)," at the Ka'ba shrine.

On the day of the memorial sacrifice in Mecca, elsewhere around the world Muslims gather in their local communities in a spirit of unity to remember Muhammad's victory, joyfully declare their oneness before God, and celebrate his bounty in their lives. The faithful followers of Islam, more than is generally true of any of the other major world religions, consistently affirm and reenergize the truth they claim through the five periods of daily prayer and a deep commitment to the other faith rituals.

Muslims are held to high ethical standards. Many non-Muslims today might wonder how, even if this was true historically, it can be true in an age of terror. The prevalence of this question today makes it a good place to start our consideration of ethics in Islam.

Jihad involves a broader concept within Islam than is commonly understood. *Jihad* is an Arabic word that best translates as *struggle*. It involves two distinctly different aspects of struggle: the concern for personal moral purity as well as the concern for the safety and integrity of the Islamic community, or umma. When we understand the true meaning of jihad, we recognize that personal moral purity is a concern of Christians as well as Muslims. Each of us must be on guard against moral drift and subtle involvement with the world's negative influences, and Islam records this as being the major jihad. Muhammad is reported to have said to his leaders when returning from defending their community, "Now we return from the insignificant struggle (jihad) to the chief struggle (jihad): concern for our own morality."

The more commonly understood way that jihad is used relates to fighting anything that may threaten the Muslim faith or the integrity of the Islamic nation. A text of the Qur'an often quoted out of context is, "Fight for the sake of God those who fight against you." The passage actually continues, "and do not attack them first. God does not love the aggressors" (Surah 2:190).

As we trace this concept in the life and practice of the Prophet Muhammad, it becomes clear that his military success was closely related to his defensive conduct as a highly moral commanding general. Muhammad carefully protected the lives of women, children, and the elderly. He never used flash-and-burn tactics to gain military advantage, because he considered property and natural resources sacred to God. Muhammad guarded the well-being of prisoners and spared their lives so they could be speedily exchanged or ransomed.

History indicates that the Islamic code of military engagement was far advanced for its time. The primary concern that brought the prophet Muhammad to the place of battle was the cry of the innocent, who were still in pagan bondage in Mecca. This is reminiscent of the prophets of Israel: "Seek justice, rescue the oppressed, defend the orphan, plead for the widow" (Isaiah 1:17).

The term "jihad" as we commonly use it today has a strongly negative connotation because the actions of terrorists over the last sixty years totally disregard Muhammad's teachings and practices. In the centuries following the Prophet's death, Islamic forces have used aggressive military tactics in the name of jihad, again in defiance of his ethical principles. This moral failure has also been true in the history of Christian leaders who have been inconsistent in following the peaceful teachings of Jesus.

A thoughtful review of Muslim teaching reveals that the reverence for life is a major focus of Islam. The images that spring from a false perception of jihad are some of the tragic fallacies that divide unaware Christians from their committed Muslim brothers and sisters, who are also victims of terrorist atrocities.

A distinction in the way Muslims and Christians express their love for God is seen in two key points of theology: the doctrine of man and the doctrine of salvation. These are highly significant spiritual issues worthy of a book in themselves, but we will deal with them briefly to provide another point of comparison between Islam and Christianity.

Christianity builds its theological position regarding the nature of humankind on the moral foundation established in Judaism. Islam, although remaining closely related to the other two monotheistic faiths, moves in a different theological direction. Whereas Judaism and Christianity appear to approach these doctrines from an experiential understanding of a flawed humanity tragically dependent on divine grace, Islam responds with a more objectively rational, philosophical approach. The focus in Islam is the moral justice of individual accountability.

The Christian sees humanity as needing a redemptive sacrifice because of the original fall of man in the Garden of Eden. Judaism responds by offering forgiveness through repentance, which was originally expressed by animal sacrifice. In modern Judaism, repentance is celebrated on Yom Kippur, the day of atonement. In Christianity, the redemptive grace of God is expressed by the sacrifice of Christ at Golgotha and God's eternal affirmation in the Resurrection.

These theological issues of the human dilemma and divine salvation are dealt with in Islam in a different fashion—not in figurative language or metaphor reflecting the divine mystery of God's grace as we find in the Gospels, but in a closely argued, rational approach of individual accountability.

Following the account of Adam's failure in eating the forbidden fruit, the Qur'an simply says, "Adam received words from his Lord, and his Lord relented toward him. He is the Forgiver, the Merciful" (Surah 2:37). In several other places, the Qur'an is very clear in setting forth the danger of sin and clearly warns of the danger of disobedience and the penalty of hellfire. A general text that deals with God's forgiveness reads: "Your Lord has prescribed for Himself mercy, that whoso of you does evil and repents afterward and does right, [for him] assuredly Allah is Forgiving, Merciful" (Surah 6:54).

In Islam, there is no sense of an inherited sinful nature. Each person is born free to choose the truth of God or to live in sin. The code of morality and the expectation of purity are as high in Islam as in Judaism or Christianity. As is true for Jews, a Muslim is forbidden to eat pork. He is also forbidden to drink alcoholic beverages or to engage in gambling or in sexual activity outside of marriage. God forgives a sinner who repents and does acts of repentance, such as offering extra gifts to the poor and returning to a righteous lifestyle. But at the final judgment, each person is judged by God regarding how they have lived, served God, and been obedient to the truth. Those who have failed receive the due penalty of *the fire*, and those who are found to be righteous are blessed with the reward of *the Garden* (heaven).

The stern challenge of Islam is the burden of freedom and total accountability. The Qur'an expresses the matter in this way:

> Every man's augury (forewarning) We have fastened on his own neck; and We shall bring forth for him on the Day of Resurrection a book he shall find wide open. [It will be said to him]: Read your book! Your soul is sufficient this day as reckoner against you! Whosoever goes right, it is only for the good of his own soul that he goes right; and whosoever goes astray goes astray to his own loss. No soul can bear another's burden. Nor do We punish until We have sent forth a messenger [to give warning] (Surah 17:13–15).

Here we see a significant distinction between the salvation message of Islam and of Christianity. A theological comment about this Qur'an text focuses on the difference:

> The doctrine of vicarious atonement is condemned. Salvation for the wicked cannot be attained by the punishment of the innocent. One man cannot bear the burden of another; it would be unjust, and reduce the sinner's sense of accountability.[6]

Marriage is the center of communal life in Islam. A consenting man and a consenting woman enter into marriage freely. To preserve sexual purity, Islam does not approve of mixing men and women in social or educational activity, and premarital sexual activity is forbidden. Extramarital sexual activity is severely punishable.

Muslim dress is simple, without excess ornamentation; men are to cover their bodies from the navel to the knees and women their entire bodies, except their face and hands. Any clothing that is skin tight or transparent is forbidden. In the United States, the wearing of the *hijab* (head scarf) by women is optional but strongly recommended and is considered a sign of spiritual maturity.

Islam teaches decency, humility, and good manners along with the claims of the Ten Commandments. It condemns enmity, blasphemy, ridicule, the use of name-calling, suspicion, and arrogance. It affirms respect for neighbors, the elderly, parents, and special love for children.

A Reflection on Love for God and a Proposed Response

It is painfully clear to Muslim leaders—such as Khaled Abou El Fadl, a professor at UCLA quoted extensively in coming chapters—that the terrorists have hijacked their faith and humiliated Muslims before the world. This admission may make caring Christians more willing to seek further understanding and more eager to participate in the Christian-Muslim dialogue suggested in the letter known as "A Common Word."[7] This letter was initially inspired by the Jordanian monarchy and was written by a group of international Islamic leaders, who in 2007 sent it to the Pope and all known Christian leaders around the world.

We now turn to a careful presentation of the historical development of Islam, beginning with the life of the Prophet Muhammad. This historical review will lead to an explanation of the manner in which an emerging distorted ideology of hate and offending historical circumstances have brought us to the international challenge we face today.

Section II–
Prophet Muhammad and His Vision

The vision of Abraham started it all.[1] Writing in *The Gifts of the Jews*, Thomas Cahill explains:

> By "it" I mean so many of the things we care about, the underlying values that make all of us, Jew and gentile, believer and atheist, tick. Without the Jews [and the Abrahamic vision of monotheism], we would see the world through different eyes, hear with different ears, even feel with different feelings … we would think with a different mind, interpret all our experience differently, draw different conclusions from the things that befall us. And we would set a different course for our lives.[2]

Whether we are aware of the reality or not, we who claim to be Jews, Christians, or Muslims all flow from a common world orientation. Our perceptions are based on a monotheistic foundation that can be traced back at least two thousand years before the birth of Jesus to the time of Abraham.

Realizing our common heritage makes it much easier to appreciate those in our midst who seem different. It is in this appreciation of human differences that we find our starting point to take seriously the command of Jesus to love even our perceived enemies. When Jesus instructs us to go into the world as his representatives, we can no longer avoid such opportunities. In this small neighborhood called earth, it is time for us who love God to respond with faithful action—an outreach of friendship and love.

In terms of gospel truth, Jesus is our model. All he did started with a difficult task: having the courage to love. We must yearn for the courage to love the alien, the estranged person, and the apparent enemy. Our challenge is to affirm the scripture that speaks a constant appeal for practical love for all. God's concern must become our concern.

In an affluent culture, there is an effective attempt to keep the desperately needy and those who are different invisible. I grew up in a suburb of Los Angeles where real estate agents simply never had a vacancy if approached by a person of color. Nor was it acceptable to hire an employee of color who might need to commute after dark. These issues were never mentioned at our strongly evangelical church, which had a thriving membership of over two thousand. The poor and the alien were invisible, even though scripture calls for their care on at least three-dozen occasions.

Today, the globe is our neighborhood, and we are all neighbors no matter our color, country of origin, economic status, or religion. In this examination of Islam, we offer a case study—one of the more challenging ones—that invites us to prayerfully explore human relationships with courageous spiritual maturity. May we joyfully join the twenty-first century Pauls who have the courage to be all things to all people for the sake of the Gospel (1 Corinthians 9:22).

This introduction to Islam is a handbook of sorts. It offers information about and suggestions of how to become a friend to Muslim people in the midst of our present crisis. As you read it, prayerfully consider the possibility of actually being directly involved.

Chapter 3

Anticipating the Prophet in
an Age of Ignorance

In this chapter, we explore the environmental, cultural, and social circumstances that were the daily context of Muhammad's early life. Carefully observing his early environment will help us understand his later influence. What was it like to live in the Arabian desert towns and countryside in the seventh century CE?

In this exploration, we will try to identify with a culture and religion different from our own. Theologian Walter Wagner defines the task this way: "We come with culturally conditioned understandings about ourselves and the faith we are about to consider. Those understandings are confirmed, corrected, adapted, or amended as we engage the other religion and its believers."[1] Simply presenting objective information about another religion is inadequate. It is equally important to make an effort to communicate the inner spiritual reality of that religion in a way that reflects what has inspired and guided its followers with such power that it has endured over the centuries.

Renowned author on world religions, Huston Smith, reflects on the challenge:

> If we lay aside our preconceptions about these religions, seeing each as forged by people who were struggling to see something that would

give help and meaning to their lives; and if we then try without prejudice to see ourselves what they saw—if we do these things, the veil that separates us from them can turn to gauze.[2]

In this spirit of openness, let us discover the Prophet Muhammad and his vision in such a way that the spiritual power that inspired him may be sensed as a living reality—not necessarily a reality we will embrace, but nonetheless a reality that has inspired countless people over fourteen centuries. As we explore the environment of Muhammad's time and his desert surroundings, we should attempt to envision what this child, youth, and young man experienced and how he responded. Such openness allows us to briefly travel to a different time and place and thoughtfully imagine life as it was then lived. This inwardly imagined relocation to the desert of sixth- and seventh-century Arabia should help frame our understanding as we read Sections II and III.

The Place: A Spiritual Vacuum

Over the eons of human history, great peoples have emerged through their identification with a place and a tradition. In the case of the people of Israel, the pattern was reversed. First came their vision or sense of life's meaning, out of which came their tradition and, at long last, the land. Their initial vision is articulated for us in Exodus 14:30–31:

> Thus the Lord saved Israel that day from the Egyptians; and Israel saw the Egyptians dead on the seashore. Israel saw the great work that the Lord did against the Egyptians. So the people feared the Lord and believed in the Lord and in his servant Moses.

It is here, in this liberation epic, that the descendents of Abraham sense their collective identity as a people. For Israel, the "fear of the Lord" was their grand vision, their reason for being. From Egypt they went forth into the desert, the wilderness of Sinai, and the wilderness of Paran. It was in the Sinai that the second phase occurred that refashioned these former Egyptian slaves into the unique people of God. At Mount Sinai, God gave them the Ten Commandments, the ethical norm for future civilizations. It was also in the desert that the Lord God gave them a pattern of worship and the grand sense of tradition that guides the Hebrew people even to this day. A sense of nationhood emerged as the Hebrew people journeyed for over forty years in the wilderness, as recorded in Exodus, chapters 20–40. The oracle declarations of the Lord equipped them to work through, and transcend the folly of, their disobedience. Their sense of identity was finalized, and Moses climbed Mount Nebo to sing his last song of celebration (Deuteronomy 32–33). It was left to Joshua to successfully lead the Hebrew people across the Jordan River and guide them as they carved out a new nation.

For reasons known only to God, future revelations of his truth were heard in different places under different conditions. At the correct prophetic moment, when the angels sang in Bethlehem, the glad news they heralded was silent on the Sinai, then and for hundreds of years to follow. A pessimistic Arabian proverb declared that the voice of God was strangely silent for them. Only evil phantoms known as *jinn* were common among the desert caravans as the Arabs made their isolated commercial crossings.

The people of the Sinai lived with their flocks and communicated across the vast spaces by means of their trading caravans. In the rare communities that did exist, such as Medina and Mecca, life was difficult and punctuated by continuous tribal warfare. Each small group seemed jealous of the bit of goods that its neighbor possessed.

The community of Mecca was favored above the others, for in Mecca there was the Ka'ba, once a visible sign of the presence of God. Mecca in the sixth century, however, had become the focal point for the tribal idols of Arabia. It was economically enriched by the clamoring pattern of competitive idolatry, but it was also diminished by the greed and brutal paganism so typical of those who worshipped wood and stone. In this sense, Mecca was the focal point of the despair of the Arabian Peninsula. Life without focused meaning, life without unifying and stable tradition, and life without the security of moral law was the fate of the *Quraysh*, the dominant tribe of Mecca.

The Jahiliyyah–An Age of Ignorance

The Arabian Peninsula was an insignificant political and social area on the margin of two great civilizations. To the northwest was the flourishing Byzantine Empire, and to the north was the great Persian Empire. These superpowers of their day were in harsh competition with each other as well as with much of medieval Europe. Eastern Orthodox Christianity was the religion of the Byzantines, and Zoroastrianism was the religion of the Persians. The Arabs had been shunted aside in the deserts of north Arabia, and they had a saying that God had left them with no scripture and no prophet.

Nevertheless, the Arabs knew that they came from a legendary figure. Abraham was not only the father of the Jews, but he was also the father of the Arabs. His oldest son, Ismael, the Arabic for *Ishmael*, was their direct ancestor. When speaking to Hagar, Abraham's handmaiden, God said, "Now you have conceived and shall bear a son; you shall call him Ishmael, for the Lord has given heed to your affliction" (Genesis 16:11).

Later, speaking to Abraham, God said:

> As for Ishmael, I have heard you; I will bless him and make him fruitful and exceedingly numerous; he shall be the father of twelve princes, and I will make him a great nation (Genesis 17:20).

Building on this latter verse, a Muslim text tells us that Abraham and Ismael went to the well of Zamzam that had initially nurtured Hagar in her desert wandering.[3] There, near the well located outside Mecca, father and son built the Ka'ba in honor of *Allah*, the term in Arabic literally meaning *the God*. The Ka'ba continues today as the focal point of the Islamic *hajj*, where God is worshipped by thousands of Muslim pilgrims making their yearly sacred pilgrimage to Mecca (Qur'an 2:124–127 and 3:95–96).

As noted earlier, by the sixth century CE, the Ka'ba had become a very different thing indeed. It was the focal point of worship of three hundred sixty gods, the tribal deities of the various Arabian tribes and their respective clans. Each year Arabs engaged in incantation and rituals to honor their gods. In *Muhammad: A Biography of the Prophet*, Karen Armstrong says, "The land around Mecca (on a twenty-mile radius with the Ka'ba as its center) was a sacred area, where all violence and fighting was forbidden."[4] It thus served as a place of annual worship as well as a safe haven in the midst of strife.

In this same period, the practice of *ghazwa* (tribal raids) was carried out in a crude way to preserve a balance of power and wealth. If a tribe was in a precarious economic condition, it was considered quite normal for that tribe to raid another tribe, carrying away whatever wealth they could seize. This concept of social justice was similar to the "eye for an eye" practice of interpersonal justice found in both the Qur'an 5:45 and Exodus 21:23–25. In the latter, we read that if any harm follows from a fight, "then you should give life for life, eye for eye, tooth for tooth, hand for hand, foot for foot, burn for burn, wound for wound, stripe for stripe."

However, there is a significant variation in the ending of the passage in the Qur'an. At the point of "wound for wound," the Qur'an reads, "and for wounds, retaliation. But, if anyone remits the retaliation [by means of charity], it is an act of atonement for himself." Paradoxically, such charitable atonement was seldom practiced. Rather, if the perpetrator of the offense could not be found, another person of the tribe was given up to the offended party and the price exacted. This is another indication of the unrest and brutality in Muhammad's time.

Male youths were trained for rigorous battle as well as an unflinching willingness to accept undeserved punishment to preserve the tribe's honor, all a part of the rite of passage known as *Muruwwah*. This practice kept the tribal communities of Arabia in a general state of intertribal tension or, on occasion, all-out warfare.

There were those few who rose above the grip of the paganism in the Ka'ba, who yearned for one true religion. These individuals were known as *Hanifs*. Although they were neither Jew nor Christian, their vision seemed to somehow hark back to the faith of their great forefather Abraham. In *The Call of the Minaret*, Bishop A. Kenneth Cragg writes, "Islam is later described as fulfilling the religion of the *Hanifs*, whose great ancestral prototype was Abraham, the hero of ancient iconoclasm in the name of the single sovereign Lord."[5] The Hanifs were few in number, yet their very presence indicated the spiritual yearning experienced among the few during this *Jahiliyyah*—the Age of Ignorance.

It is here in the desert oasis of Mecca in 570 CE, at a time of little inner peace or social order, that Muhammad was born. The baby was born into a family of frequent personal tragedy and economic stress.

The Prophecy of Muhammad

The ancestry of Muhammad's parents is traced to Abraham's first son Ishmael. Moving to the next generation, the name of Ishmael's second son Kedar is found in several Old Testament references: Genesis 25:12–16; Psalm 120:5; Isaiah 21:16–17, 42:11, and 60:7. Here we see the direct connection between the Prophet Muhammad and the patriarch Abraham, who fathered the Arab peoples through Ishmael, as the Jewish nation was fathered through Isaac.

A history rarely referred to in either Jewish or Christian studies indicates the biblical anticipation of a prophet who would come to the Arabs. As much, however, as Christians anticipating the birth of Jesus turn to Micah 5:2 and read, "But you, O Bethlehem of Ephrathah, who are one of the little clans of Judah, from you shall come forth for me one who is to rule in Israel," so students of Islam see their emerging story of the future birth of Muhammad reflected in the prophet Habakkuk 3:2–3:

> O Lord I have heard of your renown, and I
> stand in awe, O Lord, of your work. In our own
> time revive it; in our own time make it known;
> in wrath may you remember mercy. God came
> from Teman, and the Holy One from Mount
> Paran. His glory covered the heavens, and the
> earth was full of his praise.

Yes, it was there at the foot of the Paran Mountains in Mecca that the Prophet Muhammad was born. For many, this text from Habakkuk is of little significance, yet for others it is part of the scriptural heritage that identifies the place of Muhammad's birth.

In John 1:19–25, John the Baptist is asked about his identity by a group sent from Jerusalem. He is asked three questions: "Who are you? Are you Elijah? Are you the Prophet?" John quickly responds that he is none of these. Then, in response to further pressure, he tells them, "I am the voice of one crying out in the wilderness, 'Make straight the way of the Lord.'" In John 7:40–41, after Jesus had spoken near the temple, a controversy arose about his identity, and some in the crowd said, "This is really the Prophet." Others speculated that he was the Messiah. In these texts, it is pointed out that in the first century, Jews were anticipating not only the Messiah but also "the Prophet who was to come."

The significance of this for Muslims becomes clear as we recognize that their tradition not only honors Muhammad as "the Prophet who was to come," but also honors Jesus as the Messiah (Surah 9:31) and as the one who fulfills Jewish prophecy and reveals the Gospel (Surah 5:46). It is Muslim belief that both are promised, and that Gospel and Qur'an passages reflect that reality. Muslim teaching affirms that the coming of the Prophet Muhammad is indicated in both Testaments. This is another sensitive point to remember as we consider future interfaith conversations.

Born into Obscurity, Poverty, and Grief

In 570 CE, Abd Allah ibn Al Muttalib, a poor young man recently married, sought greater security for his new family. As part of this effort, he left his pregnant wife to participate in a caravan trip to the north. Tragically, during the return trip, he became desperately ill and died. A few months later, the widow Aminah bint Wahb gave birth to Muhammad. The couple had been wed less than a year, and the widow was left with few resources. Since her family came from the north near the oasis of Medina, she turned for help to her grieving father-in-law, Abdu'l-Muttalib. Having lost his beloved son, he in turn gladly welcomed his grandson.

A surprising aspect of Arab urban society of the sixth century was the desire to ground children in the fullness of Bedouin tribal culture. Parents living in Mecca wanted their children to experience the richer Arabic language of the Bedouins and to be a natural part of that ancient desert heritage. Thus, it was the custom for mothers to seek out a wet nurse in a Bedouin community to care for their young children. Young Bedouin mothers appreciated such opportunities that in later years could open connections for them with the richer, urban people of Mecca. The widow Aminah, wishing the best for her infant son Muhammad, sought to place him with a Bedouin nurse. As a widow with little promise of future wealth, such a relationship seemed unlikely.

However, some weeks after Muhammad's birth, a Bedouin group passed through Mecca. Aminah met Halimah, a needy young mother nursing an infant. This desperately poor woman and her husband begrudgingly accepted the responsibility of taking Aminah's infant.

Later, Halimah reported that she had no sooner put the infant Muhammad to her bosom than her breasts, which had insufficient milk for her own child, were suddenly full and flowed abundantly. According to tradition, the first night the infant was with them, Halimah's husband went to his nearly dry camel and found her udder large and unexpectedly filled with milk. That night, for the first time, the couple and their own infant went to bed with stomachs full and spirits contented. When two years had elapsed and the toddler Muhammad was to return to his mother, Halimah begged to keep him longer because his presence was such a blessing. Aminah graciously extended the time and only received her son back into her family when he was nearly four. This separation from his surrogate mother upon returning to his birth mother was the first of what would prove to be a series of radical disruptions in young Muhammad's life.

Tradition tells us very little of the next two or three years, but at the age of six, Muhammad experienced his second tragic loss. Aminah died, and the boy became an orphan. She had made arrangements with her father-in-law to assume responsibility for the youngster. Muhammad's deceased father had been an especially beloved son, so Muhammad found in his grandfather a man of sensitivity and devotion. The six-year-old Muhammad soon became his grandfather's regular companion. Sadly, this happy comradeship of child and grandfather was all too short. When Muhammad was only eight, Abdu'l-Muttalib also died. Thus, as a child, he experienced a continued series of losses and grief—separation from his Bedouin surrogate mother when he was four and the deaths of his birth mother when he was six and his grandfather when he was eight. These devastating experiences left a lasting mark upon the boy's life.

A Potential Faith Conversation: Anticipation, Wonder, and Pain

As we learn about the details of Muslim history and faith experience, imagine, if you will, sharing a faith discussion with a Muslim neighbor. In the Christian faith experience, both the prophetic scriptures we read and the carols we sing help tell us the "truth" within the mystery of divine revelation as we celebrate the birth of Jesus. Many Muslims are able to appreciate our joy because they also believe Jesus is the Jewish Messiah born of the Virgin Mary.

Yet the "truth" behind the mystery also divides us. Muslims join us in honoring Jesus, but they are unable to worship him as the Son of God.

There is much to gain in reflecting on the depths of our own faith origins as we discover the faith journey of committed Muslims. We may find encouragement by seeing the similar paths we share as our faith stories unfold. We may, however, find ourselves in stress at the significant differences. We can joyfully affirm our Christian position and respectfully listen to the Muslim position. It is at this point where the spirit of God can be trusted to use such conversations for healing and community building.

Chapter 4

From Childhood Grief to an Urgent Quest for Meaning

After the death of his grandfather, having never known his father, and losing his mother when he was six, eight-year-old Muhammad joined the family circle of his father's brother Abu Talib and Abu's wife, Fatimah. Although nurturing, the family was large and desperately poor. Muhammad had no sooner settled in than his uncle put him to work. Using the shepherding sense that came naturally to a child once part of a Bedouin tribe, the boy became a full-time shepherd, and maturity was suddenly thrust upon him.

A year or so after Muhammad joined his new family, Abu Talib made a business trip to the north and surprisingly took his young nephew along with him on this, his first venture out into the world. As the caravan made its way north, it made a rest stop at Busra, in Syria. Much to the surprise of the caravan leader, an enthusiastic Christian monk welcomed them to an impromptu meal.

The monk Bahira lived in a cave and studied ancient biblical texts handed down through the generations before him. These texts indicated that a prophet was still to come, presumed to be for the people of Arabia. From the elevated position of his cave, Bahira could watch the trade caravans as they made their frequent trips north and south. But this day was different. As this particular caravan came into view on its northern route to Syria, he noticed a strange cloud following over it, providing shade to the travelers below. Bahira felt a sudden intuition that someone in this caravan might be the Prophet that tradition promised would come to the Arabs.

Meeting them shortly after they had stopped to rest, the monk told the caravan leader that he would soon have a meal prepared and urged that they join him in the shade of the oasis for their noon meal. The caravan members enjoyed Bahira's hospitality, but he puzzled them. As they ate, he moved with an inquiring intensity around the small circle. He made a point to speak quietly with each of them. Dismayed, Bahira realized that the anticipated Prophet was not among them. Before resigning himself to total disappointment, he returned for a second conversation with the caravan leader.

The scene must have been much like the occasion when the prophet Samuel, in his God-given quest, sought to locate the new king of Israel in the family circle of Jesse's home (1 Samuel 16). Like Samuel, the monk felt someone must be missing. He inquired of the leader if there was perhaps some other member of the caravan. To his delight he was told, "We are all here except for a boy left to tend the camels." At this, Bahira urged that the youth be allowed to join them for the meal. His anticipation was fully rewarded. While in conversation with Muhammad, Bahira examined his head and shoulders and noted between the boy's shoulder blades the telltale birthmark mentioned in the prophecy.

Before the caravan continued north, the monk took Muhammad's uncle aside. He assured Abu Talib that Muhammad was a very special child. Bahira believed the boy was the promised Prophet who was yet to come and urged Muhammad's uncle to guard his life carefully against those who might want to harm him.[1]

Upon returning home, Abu Talib doubtless shared with Fatimah the puzzling news told by the strange monk, who claimed that Muhammad would be the Prophet once promised to the Arab people. However, this practical man of the desert, although he may have experienced pride in this affirmation of his nephew, apparently considered the matter to be of little significance.

As the boy continued his work as a shepherd and mingled with the people of the community, he gained an interesting nickname. Gradually he became known as "the trustworthy one." As the years passed, his family and circle of friends looked to him for strength and wisdom. Muhammad, however, looked inward. He was restless and filled with questions and spent his free time exploring within himself as he wandered in the nearby mountains.

Emerging Manhood and a Questing Spirit

One day in approximately 590 CE, a Yemeni merchant came to Mecca to trade. He was at an immediate disadvantage in a strange Arabic city, alone and without recognized business connections. After selling his merchandise at the quoted price, he made the agreed-upon delivery. The Meccan buyer received the items and noted that the man from Yemen had no local contacts. With the recent acquisitions safely stored away, the buyer simply refused to make payment.

The merchant from Yemen, however, was not about to be hoodwinked so easily. He quietly went about seeking the leading men in the community (the *Quraysh*) and telling his sad story. Appealing to local pride and the good business sense of the Meccan leaders, the Yemenite urged them not to allow their good reputation to be tarnished by a single dishonest member of the community. He made a convincing case.

The Quraysh leaders gathered within days in an informal council circle. Although not an established leader, Muhammad at the age of twenty was the youngest citizen of Mecca in the circle. As the small group counseled together, they formed what came to be known as the *Hilful Fudul*, the Alliance for Charity. As a practical response to his times of private meditation, Muhammad became a charter member of this community group organized to support justice and decency. The Meccan buyer abruptly paid the Yemen merchant in full.[2]

Somewhat prior to this incident, Muhammad had moved from shepherding to a position in the caravan trade. Here he gained valuable experience. As the caravans went north and south interacting as traders with other cultures, Muhammad became aware of the wider world around him and its patterns of life and commerce.

In 594 CE, an independently wealthy Meccan widow, Khadija bint Khuwaylid, was seeking a new caravan leader for her commercial trading business. Hearing of the opportunity, Abu Talib applied for the position on behalf of his young nephew Muhammad. Respecting the family name of Abu Talib and easily gaining other favorable reports about the youthful caravan worker, the widow hired Muhammad as leader of her enterprise. Thus, by the age of twenty-four, Muhammad had gained a highly responsible position in his chosen trade.

Having begun his life as an orphan, Muhammad now had achieved early success. Established in trade and an emerging leader in his community, he appeared fulfilled. Yet inwardly, Muhammad continued to be troubled. He increasingly sensed the chaotic contradictions of the brawling pagan communities around him.

When Muhammad led his first major caravan expedition to the north, his new employer Khadija sent her trusted young male slave Maysara to be of assistance. According to reports, Muhammad conducted himself with unusual skill as a newly emerging merchant. Not only were his business skills notable, but he also conducted himself with such scrupulous honesty that he gained Maysara's high respect. The notable event of the trip, however, occurred as they approached the city of Busra on the edge of Syria. At a rest stop, Muhammad was relaxing under a tree when a Christian monk named Nestor approached Maysara and asked to know the name of the young man sitting under the tree. After Maysara identified Muhammad to the monk, the response was startling. Nestor declared that one day Muhammad would be the Prophet of his people.

Some historical background gives us insight to the prophetic statements of the monks who on these two occasions anticipated Muhammad's future. Judging by his name, Nestor was likely part of the Nestorian sect that was still common in the area of Syria in the sixth century. Nestorian understanding of Christianity was still practiced in certain Middle Eastern areas at this time. Nestorians believed that Jesus was not *the* Son of God, but was God's *adopted* son. They followed Jesus as Lord but did not recognize Jesus as being of the same substance as the Father.[3] The concept of the Prophet that was to come evidently was also an understanding carried by some parts of the early Church, as cited in the texts that we reviewed earlier.

Marriage and Family Life

Meanwhile, during her caravan's trip north, Khadija herself was exploring new options at home. She realized that she had become attracted to her new caravan master, so she discussed the matter with her friend Nufaysah. They recognized that, although there was perhaps as much as a fifteen-year age difference, the unusual qualities of Muhammad might make him a very fine husband. The two of them agreed that after the caravan returned to Mecca, Nufaysah would approach Muhammad and, in the context of a general discussion, make casual inquiry about his prospects for marriage.

The caravan trip turned out to be especially successful financially. The profit from the trading negotiations nearly doubled the value of the cargo. Upon their return to Mecca, Muhammad immediately reported the good fortune of their trip to Khadija. It appears, however, that the report from her slave Maysara was of greater personal interest to Khadija than the financial success of the trip. Maysara gave her a glowing report of the scrupulous honesty he had observed in Muhammad's leadership, and then he told her of the startling meeting with the monk Nestor.

After hearing Maysara's report about the claims of the monk, Khadija had second thoughts about the wisdom of a marriage to Muhammad. At this point, she consulted her cousin Waraqa, one of the few Christians in Mecca. When Waraqa heard the story of Nestor's declaration that Muhammad would be the Prophet of his people, he responded with surprising joy. He indicated his own positive conviction about Muhammad and assured Khadija she should have no concern about Muhammad's future stability or character.

When the time came for Nufaysah to approach Muhammad, she inquired in a general way about his future intentions for marriage. Muhammad told her that marriage was impossible, that he must wait until he was recognized as financially stable. Nufaysah boldly asked whether he would feel differently if the bride was already a person of wealth. Naturally curious, Muhammad spontaneously asked her who this bride might be. When he learned that Khadija was the lady in question, he responded with enthusiasm.

At the time of the wedding, Muhammad gave his bride a dowry of six camels. Khadija gave him a young slave boy, Zayd, whom Muhammad immediately freed. Zayd was raised as part of their family, as was Ali ibn Abu Talib, the son of Muhammad's uncle, who came to the couple at age five because Abu Talib's wife Fatimah had died, he had remarried, and resources were stretched thin.

The marriage of Muhammad and Khadija was one of great happiness and mutual support. They continued their business relationship in the caravan trade while nurturing their growing family. Khadija bore six children over fifteen years, two boys and four girls. The boys died in infancy, while the girls prospered and had important future roles in early Islam. Zayd and Ali were raised as if they were the two boys the couple had lost to death. Years later, Ali married Muhammad's daughter Fatimah, and together they played a major role in Islam's future.

The names of the two baby sons who died were al-Qasim and Abdullah; the four girls were named Zaynab, Ruqayyah, UmKulthum, and Fatimah. In Arabic culture at the time, parenthood was honored by referring to the first son in the name of the father. Thus, in early literature, Muhammad might be referred to as Abu al-Qasim, meaning father of al-Qasim. This was a name that Muhammad especially appreciated later in life as a tribute to his baby son who had died.

Community Leadership and Respect

In the year 605 CE, the Quraysh community assembled the leaders of its various clans and decided to rebuild the aging Ka'ba. This was a daunting undertaking accompanied with a degree of fear and pride. The Ka'ba, in its place of honor at the center of Mecca, was deeply revered not only as a place of religious veneration but also by tradition was considered to be the work of Abraham and Ishmael. The clans selected their most trusted representatives and went to work dismantling the battered old shrine. When they got down to the basic foundation, they found it sturdy and amazingly preserved. Therefore, they rebuilt on the original foundation as a tribute to its Abrahamic origin. They gathered extra stone and built the Ka'ba higher and more secure than it was before.

As the rebuilt edifice was nearing completion, a divisive quarrel broke out among the tribal units. The source of the dissension was primarily a matter of clan rivalry and disagreement. The specific issue at stake was who would have the highly symbolic role of returning the sacred black stone to its place of honor. This stone was thought to be a meteorite and was the focal point of the Ka'ba and its cultic worship. After angrily discussing the issue for a week, in desperation they hit upon a solution. The next person who entered the sacred Ka'ba circle would be given the task of determining how the stone would be replaced.

Immediately after they made this decision, Muhammad walked into their midst. Tradition tells us that with a sense of relief they gave the responsibility to Muhammad, "the trustworthy one." Muhammad listened to the nature of their quarrel and quickly resolved the issue. He called for a large cloak upon which he placed the sacred stone. Then he asked a representative of each clan to grasp the edge of the cloak, lift the stone, and carry it to its appointed place. When the honorary bearers arrived at the newly rebuilt Ka'ba, Muhammad slid the stone from the cloak into the prepared niche.[4]

Once a pitied orphan, Muhammad was now an honored member of the community. For the moment, Muhammad was their hero.

Chapter 5

The Vision of Monotheism and Muhammad's Response

Following his marriage to Khadijah, Muhammad continued his habit of slipping away periodically to a cave on Mount Hira for lengthy times of prayer and meditation. Upon returning home, he concluded the spiritual retreats by giving special gifts to the needy.

A Sudden Intruder and a Call to a New Vocation

In the year 610 CE, on the seventeenth night of Ramadan, Muhammad was once again in the cave on the mountain. This night of prayer seemed like any other until suddenly, without warning, he was caught in the embrace of an angel. He said, "the angel whelmed me in his embrace and commanded 'recite.'"[1]

Muhammad thought the angel had mistaken him for one of the desert mystics, or *jinn*, considered in Arabia to be devil spirits. Again the angel caught him in a mighty embrace, and again Muhammad protested that he could not recite. The third time the angel caught up Muhammad until he thought his life would end. Suddenly Muhammad heard himself speaking the words that would become the first words of the Qur'an:

> Proclaim! In the name of your Lord who created,
> created man from a clinging clot. Proclaim!

Your Lord is the Most Bountiful. Who taught
by the pen. Taught man what he did not know
(Surah 96:1–5).

Muhammad was overcome with fear. He came to himself in a horror of disbelief. He must in fact have become a jinn, and the very thought filled him with deep despair. Rushing from the cave, he climbed up the mountain, no longer wanting to live. As he climbed in frantic urgency, intending to leap to his death, he heard a voice from heaven: "O Muhammad! thou art the apostle of God and I am Gabriel."[2] With this reassurance, Muhammad gave up the thought of hurling himself off the mountain. In deep confusion, he headed home.

This startling encounter in the cave was a transforming experience of the holiness of God. For Muhammad, it appears to have been a moment such as when the spirit of God called to Moses from the burning bush, recorded in Exodus 3:4. With the angel's words ringing in his ears, Muhammad rushed home to Khadijah. Upon entering his wife's room, he threw himself on the floor, crawled to her, and cried, "Cover me, cover me." Holding him, she listened as he fearfully told his strange story.

Like Jeremiah of old, Muhammad felt overcome and controlled by the terrifying wonder of the spirit of God (Jeremiah 1:7–9). Karen Armstrong, the noted expert on comparative religion, reflects on this divine confrontation:

> The experience was [terrible] because it had taken each prophet into an uncharted realm, far from the consolations of normality, where everything was a profound shock. But it was also … exerting an irresistible attraction because it was somehow a reminder of something already known, intricately bound up with the deepest self. But unlike Isaiah and Jeremiah, Muhammad had none of the consolations of an established religion to support him and to help him to interpret his experience. It seemed to have come upon him entirely unsought and left him feeling suicidal and despairing.[3]

Khadijah was Muhammad's primary source of comfort and inspiration. With amazing empathy, she seemed to know that it was the spirit of God that had met her husband. Seeking reassurance, Khadijah turned to her Christian cousin Waraqa, an older, spiritually aware man who read the scriptures of the Torah and the Gospels. After hearing Khadijah's strange story of what had happened on the Mount, Waraqa assured her of his confidence in Muhammad. The next time Waraqa met Muhammad at the Ka'ba circle, the Christian asked about Muhammad's experience and then declared, "There hath come unto thee the greatest namus (spirit), who came unto Moses. Thou wilt be called a liar, and they will use thee despitefully and cast thee out and fight against thee." [4] Then he kissed Muhammad's forehead.

It is not known if there were other immediate revelations, but we know that Muhammad, Khadijah, and Waraqa spoke to no one of what had occurred. At one point Muhammad declared that the experience was like a great wrenching in his spirit. But in time the inner wrestling and questioning began to abate, and after two years he was given a revelation of great reassurance:

> By the morning hours, and by the night when it is still:
> Your Lord has neither forsaken you, nor is He displeased.
> And verily the hereafter will be better for you than this world;
> And your Lord will surely give to you, and you will be satisfied.
> Did He not find you an orphan, and give you shelter?
> Did he not find you wandering, and guide you?
> Did he not find you needy, and enrich you?
> As for the orphan, do not oppress him;
> And as for the beggar, do not repel him;
> And as for the bounty of your Lord, proclaim it. (Surah 93)

With these glad words of reassurance, the uncertainty lifted. With a sense of confidence, Muhammad shared with family members and close associates what was happening in his life. Ultimately he felt led to enter the community and declare the truth that God had been sharing with him.

At that point, in 612 CE, Muhammad had a very modest sense of his prophetic role. He declared that his message was not new, it was simply the ancient faith that Abraham declared when he and Ishmael had built the Ka'ba. His message was not to change the religion of the one true God, but to warn his people of God's mercy, goodness, and purity.

A Vision of Glory and a Response of Rejection

Slowly Muhammad reached out to his extended family. To his great disappointment, his uncle Abu Talib and his father's other two brothers refused his message. Yet, Ali (his young cousin and son of Abu Talib) and his other uncles' sons were some of the first to join the new faith. His close friend Abu Bakr was the first, beyond his family circle, to become a Muslim. Abu Bakr immediately reached out to several young men in Mecca who joyfully bound themselves to this new monotheistic faith.

The first band of faithful Muslims included the younger members of Muhammad's extended family and other young people from Mecca, who responded eagerly to this revelation of one God. There was, however, a growing sense of stress in this circle. As the older men rejected the faith and their sons embraced it, tension erupted within families. This happened in the family of his beloved uncle Abu Talib and also in Khadijah's family. Khadijah's half brother was bitterly opposed to Muhammad, and yet this same man's son Aswad became an eager convert. This stress was also seen in the family of Abu Bakr, who with his wife and two children became Muslims while one of their sons angrily rejected Muhammad.

In 615 CE, Muhammad received a divine direction to invite his whole clan to embrace the new faith. He planned a very modest family dinner and invited all the male clan leaders. At the end of the meal, Muhammad proclaimed his revelation. However, in the midst of

Muhammad's sharing of his faith, one of his uncles rudely interrupted, and the whole gathering dispersed.

Later Muhammad bravely invited them back for a second meal. This time he finished his proclamation and asked who would be his companion in the task and become his successor. There was a strained silence in the room. It seemed that no one would respond. Then at last, his young cousin Ali, the boy who had shared his home since the age of five, stepped forward and declared that he would follow the Prophet in every way that life made possible.[5]

Despite stress within his own clan, the community at large respected Muhammad, and the claims of monotheism were well accepted. But as Muhammad explained about life after death and the last judgment, there was doubt, anger, and even rejection. Muhammad declared that since all the wonders of creation were the work of God, why was it not also within God's grace to raise the dead and give eternal life? This truth had been revealed to him:

> Is not He Who created the heavens and the
> earth able to create the like of them? Aye, that
> He is! For He is the All-Wise Creator, but His
> command, when He intends a thing, is only that
> He says unto it: Be! And it is. Therefore, glory
> be to Him, in Whose hand is the dominion of
> all things! Unto Him you will be brought back!
> (Surah 36:81–83)

Centuries earlier, Christians had received a similar revelation:

> Listen, I will tell you a mystery! We will not all
> die, but we will all be changed, in a moment,
> in the twinkling of an eye, at the last trumpet.
> For the trumpet will sound, and the dead will
> be raised … then the saying that is written will
> be fulfilled: "Death has been swallowed up in
> victory." (1 Corinthians 15:51–54)

Muhammad's revelation seemed difficult for the people of Mecca to receive. Yet, over the following year there was a gradual increase in the number of converts. It seemed that Muhammad might slowly win over the whole tribe. But in 616 CE, a crisis interrupted the progress. When Muhammad condemned the worship of three female goddesses, al Lat, al Uzza, and Manat, and demanded absolute monotheism, the people seemed scandalized. These goddesses were considered essential for the survival of the tribe. The crisis came to a head when a group of Muslims went to a glen outside Mecca to join in the *salat* (prayer), and a group of unbelievers followed them at a distance. When the faithful were prostrate in the midst of prayer, they were attacked and beaten. One of the faithful responded with violence and, in striking the attacker, blood was drawn for the first time by a member of the new faith.

Following this event, the leaders of the tribe joined together and condemned Muhammad as an enemy of the people. A strong and angry man of the tribe, Abu Jahl, along with his nephew Umar, led this condemnation of the new religion. Under their leadership, systematic persecution began. Muhammad's own people, the Quraysh tribe, were forbidden to marry a member of Islam, and trade sanctions were raised against them. Food was limited, and life in general became a daily trial.

As their life in Mecca became increasingly oppressive, Muhammad sent those who wished to leave to a Christian community in Abyssinia, and about eighty people left Mecca to escape the harassment. The Meccan leaders then sent representatives to the rulers of Abyssinia, insisting that the Christians reject the followers of Muhammad. But the Christian people of Abyssinia treated the newcomers well until it was safe for them to return to Mecca.

During this period of persecution, Abu Jahl declared a full community rejection of Muhammad. Soon after his uncle's declaration, Umar, on his own, decided it was time to kill Muhammad. One tradition has it that Umar set out with a sword to kill the Prophet. He came upon Muhammad reciting the Qur'an at the Ka'ba. Umar approached from the opposite side, hid himself under the fabric covering, and then crept around to where Muhammad was reciting. With nothing between them except the fabric, he heard Muhammad recite the Qur'an. Umar declared later that the mystery of the words overcame him, so he lowered his sword, and on that day he became a Muslim.

The power of the Qur'an seemed to exert a wondrous influence on many who heard it. Karen Armstrong wrote:

> At one level one can say that Muhammad had
> discovered an entirely new literary form, which
> some people were ready for but others found
> disturbing. It was so new and so powerful in its
> effect that its very existence seemed a miracle....
> Its verses were "signs" providing a sacramental
> encounter with God.[6]

Young Umar was not a man to do things halfway. When Muhammad left the Ka'ba, Umar followed him home. Reaching the house, Umar pushed forward, startling Muhammad. He challenged the young man about why he was there, and Umar declared his desire to make his confession of faith. Muhammad welcomed his recent enemy and offered a prayer of thanksgiving.

The next morning, Umar hurried to his uncle's home. He startled Abu Jahl with the astounding confession that he had accepted Allah and become a Muslim.[7] This was a final blow to Abu Jahl's patience. Gathering a meeting of the clan leaders, he suggested that all the other clans impose a ban on the two clans controlled by Muhammad and Muhammad's uncle Abu Talib. With some reluctance, the clan leaders put together the specifics of the ban. They would refuse all business negotiations, including buying or selling food, and deny any marriage contracts between these two clans and the rest of the tribe. This document was signed and posted on the side of the Ka'ba.

The following months became a period of deprivation and hunger. Relatives from other clans felt deeply threatened by these arrangements. It was against good sense and Arab sensitivities to see their distant relatives going hungry. Under cover of darkness, a few of the braver relatives set up a regular relief system. In time, the banned people became accustomed to this desperate means of survival.

At this point, Muhammad received a revelation that included a divine warning of God's judgment:

> Such is the seizing of your Lord when He seizes
> the communities while they are working iniquity.
> Assuredly, His seizing is painful, severe. Surely
> this is a sign for those who fear the penalty of
> the Hereafter. (Surah 11:102)

After two years of suffering and uncertainty, Muhammad's firmness seems to have been rewarded. The ban was increasingly unpopular among the clans of the Quraysh tribe. Watching members of their tribe suffer from near starvation was against the deepest traditions of their people. Led by Zuhayr, a man of Abu Jahl's own clan, representatives of four other clans confronted the tribal leaders. In a meeting assembled at the Ka'ba, Zuhayr stepped to the center, strongly denouncing the inhumanity of the ban against Muhammad and his people. As discussion progressed, it became clear the group was deeply divided. Despite Abu Jahl's angry protest, a clan leader strode to the Ka'ba to retrieve the copy of the ban document. When the document was found, the awed community discovered that worms had eaten it. Only the opening phrase *In the name of Allah* remained! At that point, by near unanimous acclamation, the ban was lifted.[8]

A Time of Grief and Renewed Commitment

Biographers have said that 619 CE was a year of sadness for Muhammad. Shortly after the ban was lifted, Khadijah died. She was in her sixties, and perhaps the deprivations of the ban sped her death. Without a doubt, Khadijah's death was a personal tragedy for Muhammad. She had been his life companion as well as his spiritual advisor.

To compound Muhammad's grief, Abu Talib became critically ill shortly after Khadijah's death. Abu Talib was not only his uncle but also his father figure and political protector in the Quraysh tribe. Those opposed to Muhammad used Abu Talib's illness to again attempt to make peace on their terms. Abu Jahl gathered a deputation, visited the critically ill leader, and asked him to use his influence to force Muhammad to compromise his radical, monotheistic position. If Muhammad would only acknowledge the validity of the tribe's ancient religion, they could allow him freedom to practice monotheism and live among them in peace.

When approached with the compromise, Muhammad again affirmed, "There is no God but Allah and you must repudiate what you worship beside him."[9] Before Abu Talib's death, although unable to embrace the new faith, he reassured Muhammad that Muhammad had been right in refusing to compromise. Amid his grief, Muhammad was deeply encouraged by this affirmation from the man he had looked up to all his life.

With both Khadijah and Abu Talib dead, Muhammad was not only bereft of emotional support, but also was in the middle of a politically dangerous crisis. He was a dissident voice in his own tribe and without an elder protector. Custom dictated that such elder protectors use the power of their clan to assure that safety and justice were given to each member. During this period of vulnerability, Muhammad's sense of support is reflected in Surah 13:11:

> For every [such person] there are guardian-angels before him and behind him. They guard him by the command of Allah. Allah never changes the condition of a people unless they themselves change what is in their souls.

At this time of distress, Muhammad had the greatest mystical experience of his life. Spending the night with his cousin who lived near the Ka'ba, he rose from sleep in restlessness and went to the Ka'ba to pray. He lay down in a shelter adjacent to the shrine. He reported later that as he slept, Gabriel approached. The angel placed him on a heavenly horse, and they mysteriously were flown to Jerusalem. Alighting on the temple mount, they were met by Abraham, Moses, Jesus, and other prophets. This holy group had a time of prayer.

Then a ladder was brought, and Muhammad and Gabriel began to climb to the first of the seven heavens. Adam presided over the first heaven, and he showed Muhammad a vision of hell. Jesus and John the Baptist met them at the second heaven. At each level, there was another prophet. At the final stage, not even Gabriel could accompany Muhammad. It seemed that he must leave behind everything, even himself, if he were to see a sign of God. As Muhammad at last left all behind, only the sign of God was present.

Some Muslims have insisted that Muhammad's night journey was made in his physical body. But in his biography, Ibn Ishaq indicates that his sources who knew Muhammad well believe that this was a spiritual journey.[10] This mystical event became a symbol of a new phase for Muhammad's mission. It marked a separation from the past and the beginning of a new and unknown future.

Despite growing concerns about the hostility of the Quraysh leadership, Muhammad began to reach out to other Arabs. At the next season of the hajj, while circulating among the various pilgrims camped outside Mecca, Muhammad shared his prophetic message with six Arab pagans from Medina, concluding with a recitation of the Qur'an. Rather than the usual hostility, they responded with excited enthusiasm. In the Prophet's message, they saw a possible solution to a crisis in their own lives.

Even though the two Arab tribes (the Aws and the Khazraj) came from a nomadic tradition, at Medina they attempted to share the settled agricultural life with three Jewish tribes. The nomadic structure was breaking down, and each of the five tribes found themselves jealously attempting to guard their few productive acres. The result was an escalating cycle of intertribal violence.

Perhaps in Muhammad, all five tribes had found a leader who could save them from self-destruction. The next year, the two Arab tribes returned during the hajj with others to see if they could build a plan with Muhammad for future cooperation. It appeared that a new door was opening. Out of the grief and pain experienced in Mecca, God was creating a broader purpose for Muhammad's monotheistic vision.

In the meantime, there were significant changes in Muhammad's personal life. He had been desperately lonely without Khadijah. His house was empty and his heart was aching. His friends suggested it was time to take a new wife. One of the travelers who had recently returned from Abyssinia had suddenly died. His widow Sawdah seemed a likely candidate. Sawdah was quite willing to find a new partner in the dynamic Muhammad, so arrangements were made.

Surprisingly, not long after this marriage, Abu Bakr came to Muhammad with a strange suggestion. His young daughter was attractive and vivacious. Abu Bakr suggested that when she was older, Muhammad might take her as a second wife. Although multiple marriages had never been a consideration while he was married to the gifted and compassionate Khadijah, multiple marriages now seemed a useful expedient as he sought to reach out to other groups and clans. As had been true in Old Testament Judaism, Arabs found polygamy a positive cultural norm. In time, Muhammad would limit polygamous marriages to include only four wives.

As anticipated, in the hajj of 621 CE, the six Arabs from Medina returned to Mecca, bringing seven other members from their community with them. In secret meetings with the delegation from Medina, Muhammad made plans to accompany them as their leader into the northern oasis. During the discussion, Muhammad carefully explained the details of his faith. The travelers responded enthusiastically, and before leaving on the journey, they prostrated themselves in devout acceptance and obedience to God. Twelve of the converts declared commitment to the Prophet with the following ethical statement:

> We pledged ourselves to the Prophet … that we should associate nothing with God; we should not steal; we should not commit fornication; nor kill our offspring; we should not slander our neighbors; we should not disobey him in what was right; if we fulfilled this paradise would be ours; if we committed any of those sins it was for God to punish or forgive as He pleased.[11]

This commitment statement offers a helpful view of the Prophet's ethical expectation of his converts. Conversion to Islam was not only the repetition of a faith statement on the oneness of God, but also a commitment to an ethical code familiar to Jews and Christians. It was basically an abbreviated form of the ethical expectations God gave to Moses that we have come to know as the Ten Commandments. Here again we see the commonality of the three monotheistic faiths.

The call to move to Medina and the directive to fight became interrelated. Prior to this, Muhammad and his followers were passive in the face of hostility. With the revelation of Surah 2:216, "Fighting is obligatory for you although you dislike it," they abandoned a totally nonviolent response. This change came in preparation for the reality that in Medina, Muhammad would greatly expand his role as a spiritual leader. He would become responsible for social peace and order as well as the physical security of the community.

When the hajj was over, Muhammad sent Mus'ab, one of his highly trained followers from Mecca, with the delegation back to Medina. Mus'ab's challenge was to share the faith of Islam as fully as possible and instruct new converts in the meaning of this spiritual commitment.

A special aspect of Mus'ab's mission was the frequent recitation of the Qur'an, as it was recognized that the Qur'an had compelling spiritual power in attracting people to a commitment to monotheism.

When the party arrived in Medina, the response to their message was varied. The Jewish tribes seemed curious but little more. The Arab tribe of the Khazraj was responsive, and many became converts. However, members of the Aws tribal group frequently repulsed Mu'sab's efforts to convert them.

On one occasion, Mus'ab was in a garden, sharing his faith with a small cluster of Arabs. A hostile Aws leader sent an associate to break up the meeting. As this man stormed into the intimate circle brandishing his lance, Mus'ab greeted him calmly. Mus'ab suggested the man take a moment to sit and listen. Then if the man was displeased, he could break up the group. If, however, what the man heard pleased him, he was welcome to stay.

At this point, Mus'ab recited a section of the Qur'an and, as often happened, the hostility of the man melted away. To Mus'ab's own surprise, the man welcomed the message gladly. When the converted man returned to his leader, the angry Aws chieftain took one look at the man's face and condemned him for his failure. The chieftain then stormed off to break up the group himself. Once again, the gentle approach of Mus'ab and the message of the Qur'an worked a miracle. The chieftan himself became another skeptic who fell under the influence of the powerful words of the Qur'an.

As the Arab people of Medina slowly accepted the new faith, they honored this developing relationship with God by bowing in prayer facing Jerusalem. After the night journey, Muhammad had begun the practice of saying the ritual prayers facing this holy city of the Jews and Christians. He accepted Jerusalem as his *qibla*, the proper direction to express praise and offer prayer to God. This was a silent affirmation of Muslim unity with *the people of the book* (the Jewish people) of Medina. Sadly, there is no indication of a positive response from the Jewish community.

In 622 CE, a large group of pilgrims traveled south from Medina to make the hajj in Mecca. Some of these pilgrims were still pagan; however, seventy-five members of this group were newly committed Muslims. During this ritual stay in Mecca, additional planning meetings were held with Muhammad. Rather than raise suspicion within the Mecca Council, Muhammad guarded his planning sessions by meeting under the cover of darkness.

When the leaders came together, twelve were appointed as representatives of their community in Medina. It was reported that the Prophet charged them, "You are the sureties for your people just as the disciples of Jesus, son of Mary, were responsible to him, while I am responsible for my people, i.e. the Muslims."[12] Having reached agreement, the visitors pledged themselves to Muhammad in what came to be known as "the Pledge of War." The biographer Ibn Ishaq quotes the following commitment:

> We pledge ourselves to war in complete obedience to the Apostle, in weal and woe, in ease and hardship and evil circumstances; that we would not wrong anyone; that we would speak the truth at all times; and that in God's service we would fear the censure of none.[13]

It is to be noted that this pledge has a different tone than the one made the year before. The initial pledge was a general personal commitment to moral conduct. This second pledge was a personal commitment to Muhammad as the spiritual and political leader of a community in the process of being reformulated. This pledge was not meant as a document intended for battle but as a seal of total loyalty. For Muhammad and his loyal Muslims of Mecca, this commitment was critical. They were now bonding to a people with whom they had no tie except a mutual commitment to God. This move was a critical departure from all traditions of the past. Both groups embracing the new faith were facing a major challenge. The pilgrims soon to depart from Mecca were making a journey from their homes, their roots, and their financial security. The people of Medina, who came to be known as "the helpers," were about to welcome strangers to their homes and accept the burden of being responsible for the safety and welfare of some seventy families.

In the process of affirming the pledge of loyalty, as the group from Medina took Muhammad by the hand, the representatives of the Aws and the Khazraj clans solemnly swore that the Muslims of Medina would give the Prophet exactly the same protection they gave their own women and children. In reassurance, Muhammad smiled and replied, "I am of you, and you are of me. I will war against them that war against you and be at peace with those at peace with you." Thus both sides were affirmed as these new "helpers" made their solemn commitment to their new spiritual leader. A new social order was in the making, and Muhammad was bonded as the expected spiritual and political leader, with vastly expanded demands beyond those he had had in Mecca. It is significant to note that here was the genesis of the future bonding of faith with politics that became a model in Islam.

A comparative historical illustration may be useful. John Calvin was invited to restore spiritual and social order in Geneva, Switzerland, in the seventeenth century. Calvin's experience was also with a disruptive, rebellious community, where he initially became an absolute ruler. After some years of great stress, he successfully transferred his absolute authority to a city council form of government. The democratic process was possible only after a time of spiritual maturation and effective training.

After the helpers returned to Medina, Muhammad began to prepare his people for an anticipated move to Medina. Those who were willing were urged to make the necessary preparations to establish new homes in the oasis two hundred fifty miles to the north. Those with significant reservations were encouraged by Muhammad's affirmation that they were free to stay behind.

During July and August of 622 CE, seventy Muslim families slipped out of Mecca in small traveling groups, taking care to attract as little notice as possible. As they made their entrance to the northern oasis, the group of helpers was ready to welcome them. They were given temporary lodging in the homes of these gracious people until they had the opportunity to establish themselves. (Similar spiritual migrations were a part of settling the original Massachusetts, Connecticut, Rhode Island, Maryland, and eastern Pennsylvania colonies of North America.)

During this transition in late August, Muhammad again faced grave physical danger. Some just wanted him to be gone; others recognized that if he made a safe departure he might pose a threat at some later time. Muhammad's old antagonist, Abu Jahl, came up with what he hoped was a foolproof solution. He suggested a clever scheme to kill

Muhammad so no one person or clan would appear responsible. Abu Jahl gathered the clan leaders antagonistic to Muhammad and proposed that each clan designate a young man to participate in an assassination plot. Thus no one person or group could be held responsible.

On the night the young assassins went to Muhammad's house to do their deed, they heard family voices within and decided it would be a double offense to kill a man in front of his own family. They agreed to return early in the morning and wait until Muhammad left his house. Two looked in the window and saw Muhammad lying on a couch wrapped in his cloak. They then crept away, awaiting a better opportunity after daylight.

What the young assassins did not know was that Muhammad had been warned. Leaving his regular cloak with young Ali, he had left the house by a back window. The next morning when Ali rose and left the house wearing Muhammad's cloak, the assassins knew they had been tricked. Since Ali seemed like one of them, they let him pass without harm.

The night that Muhammad was to have been killed, he and his faithful companion Abu Bakr slipped out of town under cover of darkness. They went south to a cave in the mountains, opposite from the northern route to Medina, to provide a greater measure of safety. There they hid and waited until a time of calm when they could begin their trip north to Medina across the desert. During this dangerous time of waiting, fellow conspirators provided food and provisions for their travel. In the midst of this tragic rejection by members of his extended family and the people of his tribe, Muhammad experienced a deep calm. His inner state is reflected in Surah 9:40:

> If you do not help him (the Prophet Muhammad) Allah did help him before when the disbelievers expelled him. When the two were in the cave he said to his companion: "Do not despair, for Allah is with us." Then Allah caused His tranquility to descend upon him and supported him with invisible forces.

Section III–
The History of Islam

As a twelve-year-old boy, I began to read the Bible one chapter a day. Encountering the adventurous saga of the shepherd boy David, I was enthralled but also confused. David became the most eminent King in Israel's history, wrote some of the beautiful poetry found in the Psalms, devised strategies of great military conquests, and exhibited sensitive political skill, but he also was guilty of misguided folly in his personal life. In 1 Samuel 13:14 and Acts 13:22, I learned one of the reasons God replaced King Saul with David: "The Lord has sought a man after his own heart." I wondered how David, with all his contradictions, could be "a man after God's own heart." In my youthful naïveté, I admired David's skill, sensitivity, and bravado, but the errors of his personal relationships stunned me.

Through years of study and increased maturity, the answer to my question gradually became clear. It was David's spirit of zeal, determination, and faithfulness in the struggle that marked his greatness. Certainly he was not perfect. He was very much a man of his own time and culture. Despite his flaws, he not only towered over his contemporaries but also showed passionate devotion to the far-reaching purpose of God. By placing David in the context of his own time, I gained a greater respect for his achievements and came to understand why he was a man after God's own heart.

In exploring the life of Muhammad, we also meet a man of his time, immersed in the culture of seventh-century Arabia, with all its harshness, struggle, and offensive social contradictions. In that setting, Muhammad emerges, despite the contradictions, not as a man claiming divine power, but rather as a man of heroic spiritual perception. Perhaps he was not a man with whom today we would always agree, but nonetheless he was a man of incredible courage, amazing spiritual depth, and transforming social achievement.

Gradually over the twenty-two years after his mystical call on Mount Hira, Muhammad laid the spiritual foundation of a new era in Arabian life. In this brief period, Muhammad's influence and teaching transformed the religious and cultural life of the Arabian Peninsula and, in the following generations, still inspires the lives of nearly a billion and a half people. As people of twenty-first century Western culture, we need to view the stress-filled events of the Prophet Muhammad's life in the context of the difficult time and desert place in which he lived. It is in that awareness that we can gain a valid appreciation of their true significance.

How does the powerful influence of the Prophet Muhammad relate to us? There is a vitally important spiritual connection: it was on that same desert that Abraham and Moses once heard the call of God. Their vital response not only fashioned the truth we experience in our own biblical faith, but it is also clearly reflected in the life of Muhammad and in the verses of the Qur'an. Amazingly, it is our common heritage, in partnership with our own deep faith, that allows us to become wise and caring neighbors to the Muslim people in our midst.

Chapter 6

From the Cave to the Center of Power

Muhammad and Abu Bakr stayed hunkered down in the cave south of Mecca while angry frustration mounted in the city. The leaders there announced that one hundred camels would be given to anyone who returned Muhammad to Mecca, dead or alive.

As the two men waited in the cave, supporters slipped out of Mecca to bring them news and provisions. Finally, after the frenzy over their escape had cooled, their guide, Abdullah b Arqat, came at night with the two camels that Abu Bakr had supplied. Abu Bakr wanted to make a gift of the best camel to Muhammad, but Muhammad insisted on buying it. Since this migration was his gift offered to God, the journey must be made at his own expense. Muhammad affectionately named the camel Qaswa, and she came to be his prize mount to the end of his life. As we shall see, she seemed at times to have a unique intuitive spirit of her own.

The guide charted an obscure course, zigzagging north across the desert. He made every effort to avoid detection by possible Quraysh bounty hunters who might still be in pursuit. After several days, they reached the outskirts of Medina, where they stopped for rest. It was there, for the first time in this new setting, that Muhammad led a small group in Friday prayers at an improvised mosque. The beginning of a new life was consecrated to God.

As the small party entered Medina, many people along the route offered Muhammad hospitality. Among those who came out to greet him and offer lodging were his mother's distant relatives who were long-time residents of the Medina oasis. In response to each of the generous offers, Muhammad politely refused. Enigmatically motioning to his camel Qaswa, he said, "Let her go her way." He had loosened the reigns, and the camel was free to choose her own direction. Finally, Qaswa stopped and knelt at a large shed used for drying dates. Since the Prophet did not dismount, she got up again walked a few hundred yards, turned around, and returned to the spot where she had stopped earlier. Without waiting for a signal from Muhammad, she collapsed in exhaustion. Muhammad then dismounted and made inquiry about the date-drying shed. He learned that it was the property of two orphan boys and that their protector would gladly sell it to him at a reasonable price.[1]

After making arrangements to purchase the shed, Muhammad accepted shelter at a neighboring home. The first order of business was to gather the immigrants who had preceded him to Medina together with the local helpers into a united project of building a new mosque. They set about transforming the date-drying shed into their new structure for community worship. The Prophet himself worked at common labor in the midst of them all. Unlike some of his Meccan followers from the merchant class, who were doing manual labor for the first time, Muhammad seemed at home in the new venture. Meccan immigrants and Medinan helpers demonstrated a united spirit as they worked. The new mosque, although simple and utilitarian, was a symbol of their growing unity.

Outreach to the Jewish Community of Medina

When the first Meccan emigrants left for Medina, the Prophet had encouraged them to make extra effort to establish good relations with the native Jewish people there. Surah 29:46 of the Qur'an illustrates his concern:

> And argue not with the People of the Book
> unless it be in a way that is better ... and say:
> "We believe in that which has been revealed unto
> us and revealed unto you; our God and your
> God is One and unto Him we surrender."

In response to Muhammad's concern, they were careful to respect the Friday evening worship of the original three Jewish tribes of Medina. They also observed the sanctity of the Jewish holy days. Their own prayers were offered facing Jerusalem; this was their *qibla*, meaning the focus and direction of prayer. These efforts were made by the new settlers and the two tribes of Arab helpers in an attempt to bond with the original Jewish tribes. Shortly after arriving in Medina, Muhammad received additional words of inspiration clearly indicating a common bond of Muslim/Jewish spiritual unity. These verses became part of the growing body of sacred truth found in the Qur'an:

> O Children of Israel, remember My favour which I did bestow upon you, and fulfill your Covenant with Me and I shall fulfill My Covenant with you; and fear Me alone. And believe in the Book (the Holy Qur'an) I have now sent down, which confirms the Scripture which you already possess, and be not the first to reject it. Sell not My revelations for a paltry price; and fear Me alone. Do not confound truth with falsehood, nor knowingly conceal the truth. Establish Salat (daily prayers), and pay Zakat (giving alms), and bow with those who bow down. How is it that you enjoin others to follow the Right Way, but forget it yourselves, though you read the Scriptures (the Torah)! Have you no sense? Seek help in patience and with Salat; and truly it is hard save for the humble-minded. Those [who are humble-minded] know that they will meet their Lord and that to Him they will return. O Children of Israel! Remember My favour that I bestowed upon you and how I preferred you above all the worlds. (Surah 2:40–47)

In addition to the new revelation and the camaraderie being developed through their work, the Prophet saw the necessity of writing a special covenant for the emerging umma (community). The document explained that the five tribal groups (the three Jewish tribes and two Arab tribes of Medina) and the Muslims who had fled from Mecca to Medina were now one people. Each one's property, liberty, and religion were to be respected and mutually guarded from all outsiders. No one could take sides supporting someone outside the community against someone who was a community member. Jews were to have their religion, and Arabs were to have theirs. All, however, were now monotheists and were to mutually protect one another from all outsiders. None were to go to war without the permission of Muhammad, but they could demand retribution against criminals among them. All were to live within the law of God and report all infractions to God and Muhammad. The poor and destitute were to be cared for. With these and other concerns, the new covenant bound them together.

Initially, the six groups in Medina seemed to accept the covenant and their new unity. This unity was signified as each of the leaders signed the document on behalf of their people. They especially appreciated the end of tribal strife, but there were indications that some who agreed outwardly and pledged themselves to the covenant still had serious reservations.

The Desperate Spiritual Challenge

In the early days in Medina, the Jews continued their traditional pattern of worship while the Arabs gathered with Muhammad spontaneously for daily prayers. However, this was proving inefficient with the growth in the Arab community. As if in spontaneous response to the problem, a member of the community had a vivid dream in which a specific person was designated to officially make the call to morning prayer. The dream even included words for the call to prayer. Three times a crier was to declare:

> Allah Akbar. I bear witness that there is no god but Allah. I bear witness that Muhammad is the apostle of God. Come to prayer. Come to prayer. Come to divine service. Come to divine service. Allah Akbar. Allah Akbar. There is no god but Allah.[2]

Bilal, a huge, rugged man, formerly a slave whom Abu Bakr had bought and set free, had a wonderful, penetrating voice. He was appointed the *mu'azzin*, the *one to proclaim* the time of prayer. He was to stand atop the highest house, and at the first sight of the morning sun, he was commissioned to make the official call to prayer.

At this early period, the community in Medina had not vested Muhammad with full governing authority. He simply served as the arbiter in the midst of strife and discord. There was plenty to arbitrate, as the sections of the alliance struggled to establish their new unity.

An awareness of the significance of their faith increased among the Arab tribes as they developed the meaningful practices of faithful daily prayer, hearing the Qur'an, and the giving of alms. Yet, that very Arab faithfulness seemed to have created increasing dissent among the Jewish tribes. The Jews had formerly held a unique spiritual position as the sole followers of the one true God. Their monotheism was a point of high prestige in Medina. As Arabs also came to enjoy a spiritual focus in life, the Jews appeared to become increasingly contentious.

Amid this Jewish stress, a powerful conversion occurred. An especially gifted rabbi, Abdullah b Salam, stepped forward with a startling admission. Ibn Ishaq, the early biographer of the Prophet, tells the story:

> [The rabbi] said: "When I heard about the apostle I knew by his description, name, and the time at which he appeared that he was the one we were waiting for, and I rejoiced greatly thereat, though I kept silent about it until the apostle came to Medina.… I was working at the top of a palm-tree and my aunt … was sitting below. When I heard the news I cried, 'Allah Akbar' and my aunt said, 'Good gracious, if you had heard that Moses … had come you could not have made more fuss!' 'Indeed, aunt,' I said, 'he is the brother of Moses and follows his religion, being sent with the same mission.'"[3]

When Abdullah b Salam gave testimony of his confidence that Muhammad was a prophet, the Jewish community cruelly turned on him and mocked his leadership. In the weeks to follow, there was growing resentment and distrust. The point cannot be overemphasized.

This Jewish rejection was one of the deepest disappointments in the life of the Prophet. In coming to Medina, he had expected that these, the People of the Book, would eagerly accept him, and together they would celebrate their monotheistic unity. From this point, the Jewish disillusionment spilled over into the larger community. Some of the skeptical members of the original two Arab tribes of Medina joined the disillusioned Jews in their disruption of communal peace. Muhammad then reminded them of their covenant commitment, agreed on shortly after he had arrived.

The tension was compounded some weeks later when a large Christian contingent from Nijras came to consult with the Prophet. Hearing of the visitors, some Jewish rabbis of Medina entered into a debate with the Christian visitors. One of the rabbis challenged the Christian guests, "You have no standing!" and he denied Jesus. The Christian leader then denied that Moses had been a prophet and that the Torah was valid. This event appears to have been a point of deep discouragement for Muhammad. Rather than affirming their basic oneness within monotheism, the groups had each repudiated their earlier points of unity and focused on their individuality, thus remaining tragically estranged.[4]

Shortly after this contentious interaction, in response to a new revelation, Muhammad made one of the most significant symbolic decisions of his career. In the midst of a prayer service, he directed all the worshipers to turn from facing Jerusalem. Without explanation, he told them to turn facing south in the direction of the Ka'ba in Mecca. Then the prayers continued. This became, and remains today, their qibla, their direction of prayer.

Muhammad later explained what seemed only natural and obvious to the Arabs. The Ka'ba was the original focus of worship in the beginning of monotheism when Abraham and Ishmael originally built it in Mecca. Jerusalem, however, did not become a monotheistic center for worship until after David declared it his capital city and Solomon built the Temple a thousand years later. The Romans had ultimately destroyed the Temple, but the Ka'ba remained. This renewed identity with the Ka'ba was a significant unifying change for the Quraysh from Mecca and the Aws and Khazraj (Arab helpers) of Medina. As polytheists, the Arabs had gone on pilgrimage to worship at the Ka'ba, but now

Arabs from around the peninsula could go there in the unity of Islam, affirming a monotheistic oneness at the place that father Abraham had originally established for the worship of God.

However, in the very act of more fully unifying the Arab tribes, the change in qibla became a point of offense to the Jewish tribes of Medina. Although they had not, as Jews, participated in the group prayer facing Jerusalem, they nevertheless sensed that Muhammad was renouncing Jerusalem as the great center of monotheism. As the Arabic Muslim umma gained strength and unity, the Jewish groups felt estrangement and dissatisfaction. In spite of his effort to reach out to all groups, the Prophet's efforts to bring peace and wholeness to Medina were on the one hand, symbolically achieved, and on the other, tragically flawed.

Chapter 7

The Military Challenge

Beginning his new life in Medina, Muhammad faced a social complexity far beyond anything he had previously experienced. The internal divisions at the oasis involved conflict of both social and religious dimensions. Muhammad approached the challenge as an idealist, with only God as his inspiration. Unlike the situation in first century Israel in the time of Jesus, there was no Mosaic code of conduct established in Arabia. Nor was there a civil code of justice similar to the *Pax Romana* to maintain peace. No matter how corrupt and subject to political intrigue first-century Israel may have been, these structures provided a sense of social stability. In seventh-century Arabia, there were no police or courts. Every tribe was a law unto itself.

Muhammad entered a Medina both in turmoil over conflicting tribal values and under threat of annihilation by Mecca. He knew that a new justice system was needed to establish internal social stability and bring about peace, but there was no precedent for how this noble social experiment could be achieved. He was dependent on his innate wisdom, the experience of trial and error, and divine intervention. The significant spiritual inspiration he experienced, in time, became chapters of the Qur'an.

Essentially, Muhammad left Mecca as Abraham had left Ur of the Chaldeans, anticipating the fulfillment of the monotheistic vision, but not knowing the conditions he would meet. Muhammad was an idealist, much like Moses had been leading the emerging twelve tribes of Israel as they fled from the Pharaoh of Egypt. Muhammad took on the task of leading an unruly community in Medina, partially aware of the Ten Commandments of Sinai, but unfamiliar with the specifics of building a unified community. Like many devout idealists, he bumped into reality with painfully mixed results.

Initially the pilgrims from Mecca had relied on the generous provision of the helpers of Medina. This support was obviously intended as a short-term strategy. To continue this arrangement would be an unfair imposition. Immigrants then, as in the generations since, find employment in a new homeland a vexing problem. There simply was not sufficient work for the influx of seventy new families into the oasis community. This dilemma pressured Muhammad to provide a livelihood for over three hundred people in the midst of the relatively small agricultural area already occupied by the quarrelsome three Jewish and two Arab tribes, plus the Muslims from Mecca. The persecution of Mecca not only deprived his people of religious freedom but also stripped the pilgrims of their homes, possessions, and livelihood.

In the midst of this resettlement crisis, Muhammad found himself pushed to take extreme action. In contrast to his previous role of peacemaker and unifier, Muhammad turned to the ancient Bedouin practice of raiding the prosperous to safeguard the survival of the needy. The raids he undertook could also be seen as a response to God's call to fight the polytheists and reclaim a measure of justice. In Surah 4:74, we see the origin of the concept that a holy war martyr will have great blessing in life eternal.

> Let those fight for the cause of Allah who sell
> the life of this world for the Hereafter. Whoever
> fights for the cause of Allah, be he slain or be
> he victorious, on him We shall bestow a great
> reward.

Surah 4 continues, giving a divine call for military intervention to rescue the remaining Muslims still under the polytheistic persecution.

> And why should you not fight for the cause of
> Allah and for the weak among men and of the
> women and the children who are crying: "Our
> Lord! Rescue us from this town of which the

people are oppressors! Oh, give us from Your presence some protecting friend! Oh, give us from Your presence some defender!" ... Those of the believers who sit [at home in Medina], other than those who have a [disabling] hurt, are not equal with those who strive for the cause of Allah with their wealth and their lives. (Surah 4:75, 95)

This justification for force later became a basic understanding behind Muhammad's transition from a passive spiritual leader to an active military commander. Like Joshua's call from God to claim the Promised Land (Joshua 1:1–6, 11), Muhammad saw himself called of God to provide a home and security for a new monotheistic society in Arabia.

Three Battles on the Way to Victory at the Ka'ba

The Battle of Badr

Word came that a major Meccan caravan, led by Abu Sufyan, a brilliant former friend of Muhammad, was traveling from Syria to Mecca. This caravan had begun its trip south from Syria carrying a large sum of money and a great deal of merchandise. Muhammad directed that a force of about three hundred men should raid this caravan. The Muslims were divided in their response. Some were eager to go, recognizing that the wealth of the caravan promised the largest prize of any raid to date. Others were reluctant, because they recognized that a raid of this proportion would generate a military response from the leaders of Mecca. Although they were comfortable with raiding, they had not expected that Muhammad would lead them into a military campaign.

Muhammad anticipated the possibility of a Meccan response to his raid on the wealthy caravan, so he organized his three hundred troops to be ready not only to raid the caravan, but also, if necessary, to fight a defensive battle against the forces of Mecca. Word soon reached Abu Sufyan that an attack by the Muslims was imminent. He promptly sent a rider on a fast horse to recruit help from the leaders of Mecca, and he also changed course to begin an effective defensive maneuver.

When the messenger from the caravan reached Mecca, the response of the leadership was overwhelming. Abu Jahl, Muhammad's long-time dominant enemy, rallied the entire leadership of the city. He led out a force of some one thousand fighters, determined to make an end of the nuisance of Muhammad's raids. They had no sooner left the city when a second rider sent by Abu Sufyan arrived and assured them that he had successfully evaded Muhammad's raiding party. All was well—the Meccan force could confidently return to the city. By this time, however, Abu Jahl and his thousand followers were emotionally primed for battle. Abu Jahl declared, "We will not go back until at least we reach Badr, have a feast, drink wine, and let the girls play music for us."

In the meantime, Muhammad's group was marching east toward its prey. He sent scouts out in two directions to ascertain where they might meet the caravan and where the opposing forces of Mecca might be encountered. Upon their return, the one band of scouts made it clear that the caravan had unfortunately eluded them. The other band of scouts reported that a large battle force from Mecca was well on its way. Hearing this news, Muhammad made final preparations for battle. He dug a cistern in the center of his camp and quickly filled it with water sufficient for his force for several days. He then sent an advance team out to plug all the wells in the surrounding area, thus depriving the enemy of water. The Muslims then sequestered Muhammad in a safe place and prepared for battle.

Catching the Meccan forces by surprise in the midst of their northward journey, the Muslims had a sound advantage from the beginning. They fought valiantly, attacking from two vantage points. Although the Muslims were outnumbered three to one, the Battle of Badr was an incredible victory. Some on both sides declared it was a supernatural victory. Both armies reported that among the Muslim forces, there were warriors riding white stallions that were impossible to overpower. They thought these were surely the angels of God.

Over fifty warriors of Mecca were slain, many key leaders among them, while only eight Muslims died. In addition, the Muslims captured between forty-three and seventy prisoners, depending on which source is used.[1] The Battle of Badr went down in Muslim folklore as a clear sign of God's divine blessing. In Islamic history, the Battle of Badr has the psychological and spiritual rallying cry similar to that emancipation of

Israel from Egypt has for Jews. As the scriptures repeatedly declare, "I brought up Israel out of Egypt, and I rescued you" (1 Samuel 10:18). It was also God who gave the Muslims the victory of Badr.

A sense of victorious triumph was not the only result of the Battle of Badr. The battle was also the source of great emotional anguish, as well as serious ethical concern. The new policy of waging war against the polytheists opened the Muslims to deep personal suffering. Although their losses were few, in another sense every loss among the enemy was also their own. They were fighting family members, former neighbors, and long-time associates. In most cases, the men who died on the field of battle were their fathers, sons, brothers, or friends. They had experienced a great victory at a deep and tragic personal cost.

When the army of Mecca fled from the battlefield, the Muslims went out checking the dead and gathering captives. In contrast to the Arab battle custom of mutilating the dead and killing prisoners, Muhammad immediately declared that the lives of the captives were to be spared and the bodies of the dead were to be given respectful burial.

Among the list of captives was Muhammad's son-in-law Abu-l-As, the husband of his daughter Zaynab. When the victorious Muslims returned to Medina, a courier was sent to Mecca with the names of the prisoners and the demand of ransom for each. Zaynab personally sent the ransom money for her husband. Along with the packet of money, she enclosed the necklace that her mother Kadijah had given her as a gift on the day of her wedding. Receiving the ransom payments, Muhammad was stunned to open his daughter's packet and find the necklace of his beloved departed Khadijah. His feelings overcame him. Hearing of the Prophet's grief, the people immediately released Abu-l-As, returning both the ransom money and the necklace.

When Abu-l-As returned to Mecca, he had a joyful reunion with Zaynab. He then declared his startling decision. He told his pregnant wife that since he was an unbeliever and she a Muslim, her rightful place was with her people in Medina. Zaynab was again deeply pained and reluctant to go. As Muhammad's daughter, her departure caused extreme consternation among the still devastated people of Mecca. When her small caravan left the city, an angry Meccan mob attacked and so frightened Zaynab that she miscarried. Although the brief encounter was tragic, her party was able to make their escape and safely arrived in Medina.

Some time later, Abu-l-As traveled with a caravan to trade in Syria. On the way home, a Muslim raiding party captured the goods of the caravan, but Abu-l-As escaped. Under the cover of darkness, he stealthily made his way across the desert. Finally arriving in Medina, he found Zaynab's home. The next morning at public prayer, in a clear voice of deep conviction, Zaynab announced that she was giving Abu-l-As her personal protection. Later that day, members of the raiding party quietly restored his goods. Once rested and revived, he safely returned home to Mecca.

Arriving in Mecca, Abu-l-As gathered the men who had entrusted him with their goods to trade and gave each the benefit generated from the Syrian caravan. He then asked if any of them had further claim to make upon him. They assured him that they found him trustworthy and generous. Then, startling the group, he firmly declared,

> I bear witness that there is no God but the God and that Muhammad is his servant and his apostle. I would have become a Muslim when I was with him [in Mecca] but that I feared that you would think that I only wanted to rob you of your property; and now that God has restored it to you and I am clear of it, I submit myself to God.[2]

With duty fulfilled, he returned to his wife in Medina and joyfully joined the umma.

The Battle of Badr all began as a result of Muhammad's attempted raid on a Meccan caravan. After all the persecution his people had suffered, he considered the raid the responsible way to seek justice. The historian Ibn Ishaq illustrated this point by recounting an incident in which the Quraysh attempted a raid on the edge of Medina. Muhammad and his men went out in pursuit; the raiding party, however, evaded Muhammad and got away. In his report, Ibn Ishaq noted the following short conversation. One of his men asked Muhammad, "Do you hope that this will count (with God) in our favour as a raid?" Muhammad reportedly answered, "Yes."[3]

The Jewish tribes in Medina, however, saw things in a different light. Although bound to Muhammad by a rigid covenant, the Jewish leaders lamented the affair at Badr. They had not endured the persecution in Mecca nor had they been deprived of home and livelihood. But guided by the counsel of the full Hebrew covenant with God, they saw the deadly battle with the Meccan force as unjustified. From this point on, the Jews increasingly renounced their commitment to Muhammad and the umma, the unified community of Medina. They increasingly became a source of dissent and division. Finally, in resigned frustration, Muhammad renounced them and advocated the killing of any Jewish tribal member who intentionally provoked trouble.[4]

In these accounts we vividly recognize our extreme distance from seventh-century values, yet even here there is a common theme—the quest for justice. Perhaps history will reflect back on our way of seeking justice through the horrors of war and regard some of our practices as primitive as we tend to see these seventh-century raids and battles.

The Battle of Uhud

Knowing that the Quraysh in Mecca were deeply shamed by their defeat at Badr, Muhammad fully expected another military response from across the desert. The Prophet set about unifying his forces in response to the Jewish separatist division in his midst. He now sought to build a deeper cohesiveness among the newly converted Arab tribes and the Muslim pilgrims driven from Mecca.

On March 11, 625 CE, the army of the Quraysh, led by Abu Sufyan, began their march north to attack Medina. Sufyan's three-thousand-member force was well organized and determined to destroy the Muslims.[5] When word reached Medina of the movement of the southern army, Muhammad called his leaders together to plan a defensive strategy. Signs of internal disunity were immediately apparent. A dispute arose, led by the younger members who insisted that the victory of Badr proved their superiority over the enemy. Eager for battle, they were ready to march out and display their valor. The older, well-seasoned members of the community strongly counseled that in the past Medina had been successfully defended, even when their troops were outnumbered, by remaining inside the superior position of their own fortifications. Muhammad agreed that this was the wiser strategy. He quietly sought to build a consensus among the leadership to guarantee the least loss of life and property.

The farmers, however, had crops in the field soon ready for harvest. They sided with the younger members of the community, not wanting a season's work to be eaten up by the invaders. Hearing this logic, the youthful members again urged that they go forth immediately to meet the invaders in the open desert. Finally, against his will, Muhammad agreed with the farmers and the young stalwarts. He then went into his quarters and put on his armor. This lengthy interaction illustrates Muhammad's surprisingly democratic approach to leadership.

On March 22, the defenders of Medina marched out and were soon confronted by the Meccan force. As soon as the large, approaching enemy army was seen on the horizon, Abu Ubayy, the originally cautious tribal leader, became furious that his advice had not been taken. Without consulting Muhammad, and in disgust, he ordered his three hundred troops to return to the city, leaving Muhammad in the open field with an army of only seven hundred.[6]

The internal discord and Ubayy's last minute retreat set the course of the day. The three-thousand-member Quraysh army inflicted a terrible defeat upon the people of Medina. Muhammad himself was nearly killed; only the self-sacrifice of four devoted disciples spared his life. Wounded, Muhammad was carried from the field. He had sustained a blow to the head, causing him to lose consciousness. He quickly revived. Abu Sufyan, however, heard the rumor that the Prophet was dead. Believing his purpose achieved, the Meccan leader ordered the Quraysh army to withdraw. The next day, savoring their overwhelming victory and learning only later that the Prophet had survived, the Meccan army returned home, sparing the Muslims another tragic day of loss.

A major reason for this military setback was Muhammad's patient attempt to build unity among the diverse groups within the oasis community. He believed the goal of unity amid monotheistic diversity to be the design of God. In this case, the effort to seek consensus nearly proved fatal. His future style of strong, single-minded leadership was no doubt influenced by this failure, known as the Battle of Uhud.

This famous battle also illustrates two other key issues—the continuing aggressive posture of the Quraysh and the opposition to monotheism in Mecca. They had driven Muhammad and the converts from their homes in Mecca. Now they were clearly intent on their final destruction. Having nearly killed Muhammad, there was no doubt that they would try again.

The Battle of the Trench

The next major attack on Medina occurred at the beginning of Muhammad's fifth year of leadership. On this occasion, Meccan forces were joined by an additional large, highly diverse coalition determined to crush Muhammad once and for all. Perhaps the greatest significance of this battle was the treachery that designed it and the tragedy that concluded it.

Jewish groups outside Medina, hostile to Muhammad's prophetic claims, slowly formed a loose-knit confederation. Their leader, Huyayy, then went to Mecca and invited the Quraysh military to join in a united campaign. In response, the Quraysh leadership asked the Jews a significant question. According to the ancient text of Ibn Ishaq, the wording of the question is intriguing:

> You, O Jews, are the first scripture people and know the nature of our dispute with Muhammad. Is our religion the best or is his? They replied that certainly their religion was better than his and they had a better claim to be in the right.[7]

Hearing of this conversation later, the Muslims were deeply distressed and astonished that a Jewish leader would claim that Meccan idolatry was superior to Islamic monotheism. The reply, of course, greatly pleased the Quraysh. They enthusiastically agreed to join the new coalition.

Huyayy then approached another large tribe of the peninsula. This group secretly pledged to join in the destruction of the monotheistic community of Medina. Later, Huyayy displayed the ultimate act of treachery, when the coalition army was confronted by Muhammad's startling defensive strategy.

When Muhammad heard that a huge army of some ten thousand was moving north against him, it was clear that his three thousand troops would be unsuccessful in an open desert confrontation. It seemed that his only recourse was to defend the city and its frightened inhabitants from within. Fortunately, the city had a partial natural defense of cliffs surrounding it on three sides. Their great dilemma had always been defending the open plain to the north.

Muhammad was inspired to construct the most unique defensive plan in the annals of Arabian history. In the sand on the plain in front of Medina, he sketched the location of a defensive moat to be built across the northern exposure of the city. He explained to his leaders that this trench must be deep enough and wide enough to make it impossible for the enemy to advance a cavalry attack. As the moat took shape, the sand and dirt were to be mounded up on the inside rim as a natural rampart, giving the archers a protected position from which they could rain down arrows on any troops attempting to bridge the fortification.

Spirits were high in Medina. The people saw the wisdom in Muhammad's unique defensive plan, and they set to work with eager enthusiasm, singing and sweating together through the days of construction. Muhammad worked among them, sharing in the task side by side. The urgency was clear, their leader was in their midst, and they moved toward their goal with confident determination.

Fortunately, the approaching confederate army was unwieldy and slow. Its several highly diverse sections lacked a common strategy. They had only one unifying goal: Kill the Prophet! Since their objective was distant, their motivation was casual, and the differences among the groups resulted in a slow, tedious march, unaware of what awaited them.

The people of Medina constructed the defensive fortification with surprising speed. For them, it was a source of amazement and pride. When the confederate army arrived on March 3, 627 CE, the forward ranks were astonished. Never before had such a barrier confronted an Arabic army. As Karen Armstrong comments in her biography of the Prophet, the attacking troops looked at the offending barrier with shock, "considering the trench to be in the worst possible taste: it was unsporting, un-Arab, and contradicted all conventions of military chivalry."[8] Never had such a vile trick been used against them. As the Meccan troops pushed forward to get a closer look, they had to make a hasty retreat as arrows came down from the earthen fortification.

The highly touted cavalry, expecting a fast, easy victory, discovered that any cavalry charge was useless. The horses simply could not jump across, and when they were caught in the bottom of the trench, the superior position of the archers cut them down in a moment. The previously confident confederate leadership retreated to a confused huddle to revise their strategy. An apparent stalemate seemed at hand as Medina was closed up in comparative safety while the ten thousand troops from the south waited in confusion.

At this point, the final treachery occurred. Huyayy, the Jewish leader who had claimed that Quraysh idolatry was better than Islamic monotheism, made his move. He secretly approached the Jewish leader who controlled the Qurayza tribe in Medina (not to be confused with the Quraysh of Mecca). The Qurayza tribe lived on the southern flank of Medina's rugged fortifications. Initially, the leader Ka'b b Asd rebuffed Huyayy and refused to speak to him. When pressured to abandon the Muslims, Ka'b declared that he had always found Muhammad loyal and faithful. Eventually, however, the two Jewish men came to an agreement, and Ka'b reluctantly consented to give the confederates entrance into Medina through his section of the fortification if no other strategy was effective.

Rumor of this traitorous compromise leaked out. Upon hearing that a Jewish leader had agreed to abandon his city and their constitutional agreement, Muhammad was deeply shaken. He sensed his forces would be too few to defend both the trench and the fortifications where the women and children were hiding. To determine the truth of the rumor of Jewish betrayal, Muhammad dispatched Sa'd ibn Muadh to confirm it. Sa'd was a perfect choice for the task. He had been a friend and supporter of the Jewish Qurayza tribe in Medina prior to the formation of the umma.

Sa'd went to the south of Medina and visited Ka'b. By the time of Sa'd's arrival, the Qurayza had united in a plan to join forces with the confederates. To Sa'd's dismay, Ka'b's Qurayza tribe had renounced its commitment to the Medina umma. Ka'b declared their betrayal with these stinging words, "Who is the apostle of God? We have no agreement or undertaking with Muhammad."[9]

This betrayal by the Qurayza, however, produced no immediate change in the military situation. Ka'b had trusted his Jewish counterpart Huyayy to protect them, but Ka'b's fearful people, barricaded in Medina, had little trust in the Meccan army. They feared that once the

Meccan forces gained access to the city they might be abandoned. So rather than moving forward on the plan of cooperation with Mecca, the Qurayza sent an envoy demanding hostages as a safeguard against their fear of betrayal. This change in the original agreement with Huyayy raised fears among the Meccan leaders, and much time was spent in continuing renegotiations. Hearing of this development of mutual doubt between the two parties in Huyayy's scheme of betrayal and conquest, Muhammad felt God had answered his consistent prayer for deliverance.

The growing suspicion on both sides left the large confederate force stalled in the plain in front of the trench. Discontent mounted as the supplies ran short. Then a sudden change in weather led the confederates to the point of utter despair. The wind began to blow a gale. The confederate tents were pulled from their stakes, cooking became impossible as the fires were blown out, and sand blinded the thirsty cavalry horses.

In disgust, Abu Sufyan, the determined leader of previous victories, finally recognized the end was at hand. The camels and horses were dying, his troops were hungry, and the Jewish tribe within Medina appeared to have broken its word. Sufyan cried out, "You can see the violence of the wind which leaves us neither cooking-pots, nor fire, nor tents to count on. Be off, for I am going!"[10] Under the cover of darkness, the disillusioned confederate army began its retreat. It was later reported that when Sufyan ordered the retreat, a colleague responded, "Every man of sense now knows that Muhammad has not lied."[11]

The following morning, the Muslim troops, also in growing desperation, looked out across the trench in wonder. The plain before them was empty! Their line in the sand had held, and Muhammad's strange defensive tactic was a success. The battle was theirs.

The Final Tragedy

Now Muhammad was faced with perhaps an even more desperate challenge. What was he to do with the Qurayza tribe? They had denied their affiliation and conspired with the forces of Mecca. The Prophet took quick action. Inspired by the angel Gabriel, Muhammad ordered his weary troops to surround the southern section of the victorious city. He then demanded that the Qurayza surrender unconditionally.

Perhaps if the Jewish tribe had done so immediately with appropriate humility, the tragedy to come would have been avoided. Rather, the Jews barricaded themselves in their fortress, took up arms, and battled for their lives.

The Qurayza successfully resisted for twenty-five days. Their prospects, of course, were hopeless. They were outnumbered and faced neighbors who were outraged at their duplicity and betrayal. Finally, overcome with exhaustion, they asked Muhammad to let them leave the city. Muhammad refused. He knew that when he had allowed other divisive Jews, such as Huyayy, to leave, they had become more dangerous outside of the city than within. Their old confederates, the recently converted Arabic Aws tribe, pleaded with Muhammad to be merciful. He asked them if they would accept the verdict of one of their own tribal leaders. The Aws agreed.

During the siege, Sa'd ibn Muadh, the Aws leader whom Muhammad had sent to discover whether the Qurayza tribe was betraying the community, had received a wound that would soon prove to be fatal. In the meantime, it was to this wounded leader of the Aws that Muhammad turned. Although the Aws tribal members begged him to judge with mercy, Sa'd saw the picture from a broader perspective. He had personally heard the Qurayza brazenly denounce Muhammad and their pledge to the umma.

The wounded man first asked his fellow tribal leaders if they would abide by his judgment. They agreed. He then turned and asked the same question of Muhammad, and he also agreed. The dying chief of the Aws then declared that all the men of the Qurayza should be killed and the women and children sold as slaves. Within days, Sa'd was dead from the effects of his wound, and the Qurayza had suffered the sentence of his judgment. This tragic end to the victory of the Battle of the Trench remains a stain on the memory of early Islam.

The Battle of the Trench was the final military struggle between Muhammad and his polytheistic relatives and former colleagues of Mecca. With very little loss of life in either army, the superior strategy of Muhammad established a clear victory for Medina. Having won the decisive war, he could now begin a plan to win the peace.

The people of Medina began to rebuild their sense of community. Small Jewish groups not involved in the Qurayza betrayal continued as accepted, active members of the larger umma. Arabs and Jews lived together under the umbrella of monotheistic unity, each group free to worship as their tradition dictated. The key strength of this emerging Islamic center of power in Arabia was social solidarity built on strong charismatic leadership, which would become the norm in future Islam.

Chapter 8

The Return to Mecca and a New Unity

The victory at the siege of Medina demonstrated a defensive strategy that minimized the carnage of usual hand-to-hand combat. Muhammad's goal was not to subject the Quraysh, his family tribe, to humiliation, but to win their loyalty and eventually unite the Arab, Bedouin, and Jewish tribes of Arabia into the larger umma (community) of God's people. As Karen Armstrong's research points out, for about a hundred years after the death of Muhammad, Muslim leadership continued to see Islam as the Arabic branch of the larger monotheistic faith.[1]

After the Battle of the Trench, Muhammad sought ways to continue unifying the tribes around Medina. His outreach included letters to two northern Arab tribes who were largely Christian. It is probable that he expected they would not abandon their Christian faith, but rather join the umma in the same collegial faith relationship held with the small Jewish tribes. All the while, Muhammad continued to explore ways to reestablish a peaceful relationship with Mecca. It was his leadership style to anticipate a new venture but remain open to God's guidance.

In the midst of this time of anticipation, Muhammad had a vivid dream in which Medinan pilgrims were making a pilgrimage to Mecca. The Prophet saw himself standing in the Ka'ba, holding the key to the shrine in his hand. When he awoke, he was filled with a reassuring sense of victory. Surah 48 appears to reveal an affirmation of this vision:

> Indeed Allah had shown His Messenger a true
> vision, according to the truth: "You will surely
> enter the Inviolable Place of Worship, if Allah
> wills, in full security; you will have your heads
> shaved, your hair shortened, and you will have
> nothing to fear. He knows what you do not
> know. Therefore, He granted you this near
> victory before [the fulfillment of the vision]."
> (Surah 48:27)

The next morning Muhammad shared his dream and invited the
Medina community to prepare for the pilgrimage to Mecca. It was
recognized that such a venture posed great danger. They would be
traveling as unarmed pilgrims vulnerable to attack. Nevertheless, a
thousand responded and agreed to go on this journey of faith.

Muhammad traveled with his wife Umm Salamah, a woman
of unusual wisdom. Included in their hasty preparations were the
decorations for seventy ceremonial camels to be sacrificed as a special
offering to God in the holy area that surrounded the Ka'ba. Muhammad
dressed in a two-piece white garment of unstitched cloth, just as he had
seen himself in the dream. One piece was bound around his waist and
the other draped over his shoulders. (This simple white garment is
required of all pilgrims even today, thus removing all traces of economic
or ethnic differences and creating an amazing bond of unity.)

At the last stop before entering the holy area, Muhammad sacrificed
one of the ceremonial camels and uttered the ancient cry of the pilgrim,
"Here I am, O God, at your service."

When the leaders of Mecca heard of the approach of a thousand
pilgrims from Medina, they found themselves in a difficult cultural
bind because whatever they did could result in humiliation. Refusing
pilgrims entrance to Mecca would be a scandalous betrayal of their
sacred duty as guardians of the Ka'ba. Yet if they allowed Muhammad to
worship the monotheistic God with a thousand pilgrims from Medina,
it would be a Muslim victory that would be discussed by people across
the peninsula.

Finally, with only a single dissenting voice, the leaders of Mecca
made their decision. With indignant defiance, they refused the Medinan
pilgrims access to the Holy City. They sent a troop of two hundred well-

armed cavalry to prevent the defenseless Muslims from completing their pilgrimage. When Muhammad heard of the approaching Quraysh force, he was deeply disappointed. Yet, strong in his resolve, he confidently declared, "I will not cease to fight for the mission with which God has entrusted me until He makes it victorious or I perish."[2]

Muhammad had been confident that his dream meant he was assured a safe pilgrimage for all his people. However, the appearance of the cavalry seemed to deny the validity of his vision. The trusted caretakers of the Ka'ba were violating all ancient Arab precedent. In the face of this jolting disappointment, Muhammad again responded with creative determination. The Medinans found a local guide to lead them on a rugged detour through the mountains to the outer edge of the sanctuary, where all violence was forbidden. The Meccan cavalry was unaware of the Medinans' location until they had safely arrived at a place within the edge of the sanctuary called Hudaybiya. As they reached this safe area, suddenly Qaswa, Muhammad's trusted mount, fell to her knees and refused to go farther. Muhammad considered this a sign that they should camp where Qaswa had knelt in exhaustion.

As they dismounted, some objected, saying that this was a poor place to camp since there was no water. Muhammad had one of his companions push an arrow into a long-dry water hole, and water came gushing up in abundance. (Moses, in similar desperation, had called forth water by striking a rock in this same vast desert (Exodus 17:6).)

With the camels properly watered and resting, Muhammad settled himself on the outer edge of this desert sanctuary and waited for the response of the leaders of Mecca. He assured his disappointed and restless people that their purpose now was to wait and then calmly do whatever was needed to gain reconciliation, not war. As they waited, the air was heavy with uncertainty. Whatever would occur next was known only to God.

As word of this stalemate spread, the Bedouin tribes in the area, and even many of the younger generation of Mecca, judged Muhammad as spiritually correct. The Quraysh leaders, however, vowed that though Muhammad claimed to come in peace, they would maintain their military stand between him and the Ka'ba.

Soon after Muhammad took up his determined sit-in outside Mecca, Budayl ibn Warqu, the chief of the Khuza'ah, a Bedouin tribe, arrived. When he heard of the total refusal of the Quraysh to admit these pilgrims to the Ka'ba, he pledged that his tribe, being based nearby, would keep the Muslims supplied with food and information as long as they wished to remain. He then went into Mecca and bitterly complained to the Quraysh about their failure as proper custodians of the sacred shrine during the holy season. The Quraysh soon decided that they should attempt a compromise.[3]

While all this was taking place in Mecca, Muhammad decided to send his own envoy into the city. After some consideration, he chose to send Uthman ibn Affan, his son-in-law and a man influential among the upper social group of the Quraysh. The Meccan senate welcomed Uthman but attempted a divisive tactic: they invited him to perform the sacred ritual at the Ka'ba. Uthman refused, declaring he would never observe the Ka'ba ritual before Muhammad did. In retaliation, the Meccan leaders kept him as a hostage while sending word back that Uthman had been killed.

This was devastating news for Muhammad. He had come to Mecca, assured by his dream that he was to receive a victory from God. Now, in deep grief, he was overwhelmed by a sense of failure. This was a critical moment in the Prophet's life. It appeared as one of those rare occasions in the life of a prophetic figure when everything seemed to be hanging in the balance. Like the moment when Moses came down from Mount Sinai and found Aaron and the people worshipping the golden calf, the divine vision seemed lost.

For those who are guided by faith in the one true God, it is important that we closely observe what occurred at this critical juncture in the Prophet Muhammad's life. It gives us an opportunity to witness a deep sense of the spirit that motivates true Muslim faith.

After an extended time alone in silent meditation, Muhammad summoned the entire body of pilgrims. They came, disillusioned and dejected. Muhammad ended a short exhortation by appealing to them to come individually and make a special oath of allegiance. Without needing further explanation, the pilgrims came one by one, each taking Muhammad's hand and solemnly recommitting their future to his care.

In retrospect, it is clear. This was a defining moment in the history of Islam. At this solemn time of recommitment, the enemy was near, the vision to reach the Ka'ba was uncertain, and what would happen next was unknown. Only God knew what this day would mean—a reversal, a contradiction of their former approach to victory, and an illustration of the deeper spiritual logic of Islam. It would be through united commitment before God that the Arabs would peacefully achieve their goal of monotheistic unity.

After each of the one thousand pilgrims, including the rebel leader ibn Ubayy, who had deserted Muhammad at Uhud, had pledged their ultimate loyalty, events took a different turn. First, word came that Uthman had been held prisoner but not killed. Then across the desert a new envoy approached from Mecca. The leader of the three-man negotiating team was Suhayl, a devout pagan who, like the Prophet, had on occasion made isolated spiritual retreats.[4]

Muhammad and Suhayl sat together for a long, anguished discussion. Each man appeared to be doing what seemed impossible, seeking to understand the situation of the other while remaining true to the integrity of his own people. At last they finished, exhausted, but convinced they had crossed a great chasm with no guarantee of a safe return.

Incredibly, Muhammad had promised that the pilgrims would now return to Medina without having visited the Ka'ba. In return, Suhayl had agreed that at the same time the following year, the entire Meccan community would vacate the city for three days and give the Muslims full access to celebrate the rites of their monotheistic faith at the historic shrine.

In addition to solving the current crisis, the agreement also pledged the two communities to a truce for ten years. The Muslims would no longer raid the Meccan caravans, converts to Islam from Mecca would no longer be welcomed to the umma without the agreement of their Quraysh guardian, and Muslims from Medina who might defect to Mecca would not need to be returned. Finally, all Bedouin loyalty agreements were canceled, and these tribal people were free to make alliances with either Mecca or Medina.

When the terms were read to them, the pilgrims' immediate response was a sense of betrayal. They had spent years waiting for the opportunity to return to the Ka'ba, and once again they were refused. They had made great sacrifices, lost members of their families in battle, and waited here in humiliation for days. How could Muhammad agree to such a dishonorable peace? Above all, why would Muhammad agree to return new converts when the Quraysh did not need to return deserters?

As the agreement was being signed, the consternation of the pilgrims suddenly exploded in righteous rage. Just then, like an apparition out of the desert, Suhayl's own son Abu Jandal appeared. Hobbled by fetters, he struggled on foot across the sand. He had escaped from Mecca and came to declare himself a convert to Islam.

In humiliated rage, Suhayl jumped up and grabbed his son roughly by the collar. He then bitterly declared, "Our agreement with you, Muhammad, was concluded before this man came to you." The pilgrims looked on horrified as Muhammad agreed that Suhayl's words were true. As the young man was dragged away, the pilgrims heard him shout at the top of his voice, "Am I to be returned to the polytheists, O Muslims, that they may entice me from my religion?"

Muhammad called out after him, "O, Abu Jandal, be patient and control yourself, for God will provide relief and a means of escape. We and they have invoked God in our agreement, and we cannot deal falsely with them."[5]

To Muhammad's young companion Umar, this was a degradation of all that the monotheistic community stood for. Expressing the anguish of many, Umar challenged the Prophet to his face, "Did you not promise that we would worship in Mecca as pilgrims?"

Muhammad quietly answered, "Yes, I did, but did I promise that we would do it this year?"

Forced to agree, Umar contained himself while Muhammad went on to remind him of their binding commitment. "I am God's messenger. I will not go against his commands, and He will not make me the loser!" Although perplexed, Umar regained his composure and joined Abu Bakr, Ali, and others in signing the treaty.

On the return journey to Medina, Muhammad, devastatingly disappointed by his failure and the pain of his disillusioned followers, was blessed by a divine revelation. This special section of the Qur'an is known as the Surah of Victory. It offers a symbolic interpretation of what the Muslims had experienced as a deep humiliation by the rebuff of the Quraysh:

> We have indeed given you a manifest victory,
> that Allah may forgive you of your sin that
> which is past and that which is to come, and
> may perfect His favour upon you, and may
> guide you on a right way.… He it is who sent
> down tranquility into the hearts of the believers
> so that they may have more Faith added to their
> Faith. (Surah 48:1–4)

Historian Ibn Ishaq comments on Muhammad's apparent humiliation by saying that humble openness in seeking reconciliation was to be Muhammad's greatest victory.[6] This illustration of humility is a corollary to the teaching of the Hebrew prophets and of Jesus: "What does the Lord require of you but to do justice, and to love kindness, and to walk humbly with your God?" (Micah 6:8), repeated in the Gospels, "Blessed are the poor in spirit, for theirs is the kingdom of heaven. Blessed are those who mourn, for they will be comforted. Blessed are the meek, for they will inherit the earth" (Matthew 5:3–5).

In our own fearful age of war and terror, we need to courageously reclaim this common monotheistic heritage. The Islamic scholar Seyyed Hossein Nasr affirms this as he quotes a prophetic *Hadith*, an inspired text honored in Islam but not found in the Qur'an: "Shall I inform you of a better act than fasting, alms, and prayer? Making peace between one another: Enmity and malice tear up heavenly rewards by the roots."[7] As Jews, Christians, and Muslims, we have a great common heritage. Let us dare to live and affirm it boldly. Peace is our common goal, and we affirm the possibility that Jesus and Muhammad are potential partners for peace.

The Return Pilgrimage to Mecca

March of 629 CE was the appointed time for the promised safe pilgrimage to Mecca in accordance with the treaty sealed at Hudaybiya. For this grand occasion, some twenty-six hundred pilgrims made careful preparation. With eager anticipation as well as a note of uncertainty, they returned across the desert to Mecca. Faithful to the agreement, the Quraysh abandoned their homes and left Mecca for the three-day religious retreat of the Muslims to the Ka'ba. As the Muslims moved into Mecca, the distressed Quraysh leaders looked down from the bluffs around their city and watched in wonder as the white-clad pilgrims entered the sacred Ka'ba area to the resounding cry, "Here I am at your service, O Lord." Then, led by the Prophet Muhammad riding Qaswa, they made the circumambulation seven times around the Ka'ba and observed the other traditional ceremonies of the hajj, all done to the glory of the one and only God of the universe.

Much to the surprise of the disorderly Quraysh, by nightfall after three days, the twenty-six hundred pilgrims left Mecca in quiet, well-disciplined columns. The entire event had been a moral triumph for Muhammad and his people. Their spirits had been restored. Their influence among the curious Bedouin tribes had been bolstered, and the people of Mecca were filled with a sense of awe at the spiritual dedication and unity of the Muslims. Several of the Quraysh were convinced that they wanted to make the *hijra* to Medina and embrace the truth of monotheism. Muhammad's earlier humbling commitment to seek victory by the slow and painful means of interaction and dialogue was firmly vindicated.

In November of 629 CE, one of the Quraysh confederate tribes attacked a tribe loyal to Medina. This unprovoked attack was a violation of Muhammad's treaty with Mecca and called for a serious military response.

Abu Sufyan, a chief of Mecca, hurried to Medina, attempting to broker arrangements for peace. There he offered the first phrase of the Islamic pledge of loyalty, "There is no god but God!" Before Sufyan left Medina, he was offered an opportunity, if the occasion arose, to serve as an intermediary accepting the Meccan surrender. This would be a face-saving gesture, allowing the people of Mecca to surrender to Sufyan rather than to Muhammad.

Moving out in support of their offended ally, the Medinan army, now joined by affiliated Bedouin tribes, swelled to ten thousand men. As they moved south toward Mecca, it was immediately clear that Meccan resistance was futile. Except for one token scrimmage at the edge of the city, the Muslim army marched into Mecca unopposed. Many on both sides viewed this as a day of victory when God, in his own time and way, had restored the Prophet and claimed Mecca for himself. As the Qur'an states, there is no compulsion in religion. On this day of renewal, Muhammad sought to offer reconciliation and peace. The city had surrendered to the Medinan army, but each person individually must be free to surrender to God.

After he rested, Muhammad prayed and then, mounting Qaswa, rode around the Ka'ba seven times, crying out, "al-Llahu Akbar (God is the greatest)!" As the ten thousand troops echoed the cry, "the whole city resounded with the words that symbolized this final victory of Islam."[8] When the seven-fold circumambulation was finished, Muhammad set himself to the task of destroying the three hundred sixty pagan images that adorned the Ka'ba. Many people of Mecca must have watched in fear and awe as each idol was destroyed with the recitation of the words, "And say: Truth has come and falsehood has vanished away. For falsehood is ever bound to vanish" (Surah 17:81).

Within, on the walls of the Ka'ba, were pictures and symbols of various deities. Muhammad also had these removed or destroyed, although he allowed the frescoes of Jesus and Mary to remain. In later years, all images representing spiritual truth were destroyed, as they were declared to be distractions from the all-encompassing unity of the divine nature.

Ibn Ishaq reports that when the idols were destroyed, Muhammad's address to the people included a section from the Qur'an:

> O Quraysh, God has taken from you the haughtiness of paganism and its veneration of ancestors. Man springs from Adam and Adam sprang from dust. Then he recited to them this verse: "O men We created you from a male and female and made you into peoples and tribes that you may know one another: of a truth the most noble of you in God's sight is the most pious" (Surah 49:13). Then he added, "O, Quraysh, what do you think that I am about to do with you?" They replied, "Good. You are a noble brother, son of a noble brother." He said, "Go your way for you are the freed ones."[9]

The Final Victory: Community and Peace

Muhammad's peaceful victory and the new bond with Medina actually seemed a source of relief to the Meccan people. Some were jubilant, for now their deep but hidden commitment to monotheism could be freely celebrated. Also, the many tragically strained family ties they had endured over the past ten years were healed.

As it turned out, the new Mecca/Medina bond came just in time. The people of Thaqif, the final, large pagan settlement on the peninsula, were determined that the fate of Mecca and its three hundred sixty gods would not befall them and dethrone their goddess, Queen al Lat. A force of twenty thousand men came to fight in her defense. At first, the battle seemed all but lost for the Muslims. Then, at a critical moment, the combined Mecca and Medina forces made a successful counterattack. Overcome, the Thaqif force was routed. Then and in the years that followed, this united monotheistic power base proved victorious.

Over the years of hostility, Abu Sufyan, the Meccan military leader, had defied Muhammad with the name of the goddess al Lat on his lips. Now, as a convert to Islam, Abu Sufyan was given the honor of destroying this idol, an action that symbolized the end of pagan worship on the Arabian Peninsula.

In the next two years, one group after another among the remaining scattered tribes on the Peninsula came and made their pledge of loyalty to the umma. They were required to destroy their idols, pay their *zakat* (the money used for the support of the poor), and engage in the daily prayers. Yet, as these various tribal groups made their commitment to Islam, they still held differing spiritual understandings. Muhammad's design was to achieve political unity and trust, trusting that the virtues of the spiritual truth and the peace of Islam would, in time, result in full conversion and a common faith. This broad theological and cultural diversity within the larger umma resulted in a serious lack of internal unity in the years immediately after the Prophet's death.

A Pause for Reflection

In 610 CE, in response to his first revelation in the cave on Mt. Hira, Muhammad sought to achieve his vision for a monotheistic, united Arabia with caution in response to the chaotic social disorder around him. As reflected in the Qur'an, Muhammad's spiritual vision was structured on the monotheistic worldview of Abraham and Moses. It is worthy of note that Abraham is mentioned seventy times in the Qur'an and Moses is named in thirty-four of the 114 Surahs. This is one of several indications that Muhammad did not believe it was his calling to create a new religion, but to correct and build on the divine revelation of the past, creating a new monotheistic society on the Arabian Peninsula.

Twelve years later, on the morning of September 4, 622 CE, Muhammad completed the hijra, his move from Mecca to Medina. Several years earlier, he had left Mecca as a fugitive with a price on his head. Yet, in ten tumultuous years, Muhammad had gained an overwhelming victory over Mecca. The entrenched pagan worship and its destructive culture were defeated by superior moral, political, and military effort. As Bishop A. Kenneth Cragg, the noted Christian scholar of Islam, puts it, "That 'manifest victory' emphatically sealed a religio-political pattern as the very theme of Islam."[10] Variations of this theme are visible down through Islamic history and play a significant ideological role as Islam seeks its place in modern history.

Established when it was, this so-called religio-political pattern would seem only natural. The kings of Western nations of the time were part of an emerging Christendom ruled by sovereigns wielding power under the Old Testament concept of the divine right of kings. In both East and West, the logic of monotheism originally granted temporal power to those leaders who were, according to this concept, guided by divine power. Whereas the West moved out of this pattern into various forms of constitutional democracy, this older religio-political pattern continued in many Islamic countries, often perceived as an essential ingredient of full Islamic orthodoxy.

We see this pattern as a consistent part of the emerging structure of Islamic advance up through the Ottoman Empire. It continues today as an assumed reality in Saudi Arabia and recently in Iran, as well as in a benevolent form in Jordan. It is a serious matter of internal concern for such countries as Turkey, Egypt, Pakistan, and Indonesia. In addition, it is a muffled, or feared, concern in some Western countries that have a growing Islamic population.

This very issue is one of the strident demands of Osama bin Laden, declared in his ultimatum to the West following the tragedy of 9/11. His stated goal is for all the lands formerly under Islamic jurisdiction to be returned to their former religio-political domain. More recently, on June 2, 2008, Iranian President Mahmoud Ahmadinejad repeated his vision of the death of the Israeli regime. In a speech two days later, he indicated that he envisioned a world without the United States. These two militant points of view, one Sunni and the other Shi'a, are the primary voices in the larger Islamic struggle for political and religious clarity as they seek a new definition of their place in the twenty-first century community of nations.

A Transfer of Leadership

The conquest of Mecca was the ultimate outcome of Muhammad's efforts over the years since the first hijra took him to Medina in 622 CE. At last, in time and place, Muhammad's prophetic vision was a reality across Arabia. Quickly following the victory uniting Medina and Mecca, Muhammad was able to unify the tribal factions of the entire Arab Peninsula. The effort had been extreme, and Muhammad was increasingly conscious of his age and waning vitality. In February of 632 CE, he determined that he would lead the community on the annual hajj pilgrimage of that year; perhaps it would be his last opportunity.

On the third of March, with his entire extended family and a great crowd of pilgrims, Muhammad again entered Mecca, raising the ancient pilgrim cry, "Here I am, at your service, O God." He led his people through the old rites, treasured by Arabs of past generations, offering his people a meaningful continuity with their heritage, empowered by a new monotheistic significance. They came from across Arabia and beyond as a united community with a single spiritual focus, as described in Surah 2:46: "Those [who are humble-minded] know that they will meet their Lord and that to Him they will return."

No doubt for Muhammad this was a powerful occasion on two levels. First, it was a grand, peaceful climax of his goal; he at last saw his people united in peace in the presence of God, as fulfillment of his original call in the cave. Second, as he became increasingly aware of his weakness, perhaps it was also an anticipation of his own death and his welcome into the presence of God.

Part of the hajj ritual is a stop at three pillars near Mount Ararat where, after an all-night vigil, the pilgrims throw pebbles as a reminder of their struggle (*jihad*) against temptation and sin. Then, there is the sacrifice of an animal (usually a sheep or goat) in memory of God's provision of a substitute sacrifice at the point when Abraham was obediently ready to sacrifice his son. Then comes the great mass of white-clad pilgrims gathered reverently, circling the Ka'ba. In the hajj, we see a Muslim expression of the faith journey to God. It is here that Muslims clearly express the awareness of spiritual need and the promise of God's gift of an eternal destiny. In one sense, the hajj experience offers a spiritual awareness of our deep human need for forgiveness and renewed wholeness. The drama of the hajj expresses aspects of humility and emerging victory that we as Christians experience in Good Friday and the great, united triumph of Easter morning.

Near Mount Ararat, Muhammad gave the people a stirring sermon, later known as his Farewell Sermon. He urged them to affirm justice, end ancient blood feuds against one another, treat women with gentleness, and affirm their single brotherhood in the umma. The old tribal loyalties were ended, and every Muslim was now another Muslim's brother.

The Final Days

One day at morning prayers after their return from Mecca, Muhammad added a significant line to his prayer for the day, "God has given one of his servants the choice between this world and that which is with God and he has chosen the latter."[11] Those close to him appeared to have resisted the clear signs of his approaching death. The umma was so dependent on him that life beyond the Prophet's life seemed incomprehensible. As Muhammad became increasingly weak, Abu Bakr took his place in leading prayers. This appears to be the only hint that Muhammad gave the community regarding who should succeed him as their leader.

On June 8, 632 CE, after an extended time of illness, Muhammad unexpectedly came to the mosque during the morning prayers. He appeared refreshed and much better. Abu Bakr motioned to him to continue leading the prayers, but Muhammad put his hands up, urging Abu Bakr to continue. After the prayer service, he returned to Aisha's hut and, to her great dismay, he died in her arms. Aisha sounded the traditional Arab lament for the dead. The other wives joined in, and word spread quickly through the oasis.

The people rushed to the mosque. After affirming Muhammad's death, Abu Bakr quoted a verse of the Qur'an revealed at an earlier time, when Muhammad was thought to be dead during the battle of Uhud.

> Muhammad is but a messenger; and messengers
> have passed away before him. Will you, when
> he dies or is slain, turn back on your heels (*go*
> *back to your old religion*)? He who turns back
> does not hurt Allah. And Allah will reward the
> thankful. (Surah 3:144)

Muhammad's death was a devastating blow, not only to his household but also to the entire community. They were dependent upon him as spiritual guide, arbiter, and judge, and as their leader in all affairs, civil and economic. Although it was to Muhammad that God had delivered the truth of Islam, it was the five pillars that gave the people clear guidance how to keep their lives daily focused on God.

The critical issue that Muhammad left unresolved was the question of political leadership. The loyalty of the community was split. Muhammad's immediate family expected that Ali—Muhammad's cousin and son-in-law, and father of his grandson—was the natural leader in terms of blood ties. The helpers, the original inhabitants of Medina, naturally reached out to their own early leader, Si'd ibn Ubadah. Ultimately, however, the majority agreed that Abu Bakr was the most mature and trusted successor. Umar confirmed this choice, and eventually Si'd ibn Ubadah did the same. Although disappointed, Ali also affirmed this decision, and it became unanimous.

Abu Bakr, elder statesman of the Prophet's companions, sealed the reality of his new leadership role with a short but wise acceptance proclamation:

> I have been given authority over you but I am
> not the best of you. If I do well, help me, and
> if I do ill, then put me right. Truth consists in
> loyalty and falsehood in treachery. The weak
> among you shall be strong in my eyes until
> I secure his right if God will; and the strong

among you shall be weak in my eyes until I wrest the right from him. If a people refrain from fighting in the way of God, God will smite them with disgrace. Wickedness is never widespread in a people but God brings calamity upon them all. Obey me as long as I obey God and His apostle, and if I disobey them you owe me no obedience. Arise to prayer. God have mercy on you.[12]

Chapter 9

Islamic History after Muhammad

Muhammad had faced general social chaos as he began his ministry, first in Mecca and later in Medina. Out of necessity, much of his energy had been devoted to creating a social context in which the monotheistic vision of Abraham and Moses could be heard and expressed. This required nothing less than a fundamental social transformation, and it took effective military action to bring about.

As reported in the Old Testament, Joshua had faced a similar challenge and employed the same means. It was only after Joshua's army crossed the Jordan River to take Canaan in about 1150 BCE that a stable, cultural environment conducive to monotheism could be established there.

During the ministry of Jesus, the Palestinian people had already passed through that initial social processing several centuries earlier. Although Roman rule was repressive to first-century Jews, the rule of law we now call the *Pax Romana* created a time of international stability. Also, the Torah defined ethical stability in Palestine and, although enforced by the Pharisees in a repressive manner, it kept immorality and social anarchy in check.

The chaotic sociological pattern in Arabia during Muhammad's time required the emergence of Islam through what Bishop A. Kenneth Cragg calls a religio-political system,[1] enforced by methods similar to those used earlier by Joshua. Karen Armstrong expresses this concept:

By the year 632 it seemed as though God's will was really about to be done in Arabia. Unlike so many of the earlier prophets, Muhammad had not only brought individual men and women a new personal vision of hope, but he had undertaken the task of redeeming human history and creating a just society which would enable men and women to fulfill their true potential.[2]

Muhammad's First Successors

The Prophet Muhammad had expanded his dream for monotheistic community step by step, relying on God's direction and the power of his own charismatic vision. His death left not only a spiritual vacuum, but also a political void. Once Muhammad was gone, it would be left to others to carry this grand vision forward.

Muhammad's first four successors (the *Rashidun Caliphate*) were his personal companions in life and therefore seemed to be in a unique position to continue implementing his leadership style. It would appear, however, that the Rashiduns' bonds with the Prophet and his message of submission to God were obscured by their human quest for power and acquisition. In the twenty-nine years that the Rashidun leadership reigned, they extended the territorial influence of Islam in a sweep west across North Africa, east through Mesopotamia and into Persia, as well as north to Armenia and the southern shores of the Black Sea.

The history of this period shows that the first four caliphs lost sight of the divine origins of Muhammad's teachings and therefore failed miserably in terms of the high ethical standards required of all Muslims. Circumstance and the political considerations of the moment apparently overrode the central vision of God, as we see happening again today among the radicals who falsely claim to act on behalf of Islam. Certainly Islamic history is not alone in this regard; the same pattern is seen in full measure in the advance and conquests of Christian monarchs and republics throughout the ages.

Abu Bakr, the First Caliph, 632-634 CE

Abu Bakr, Muhammad's father-in-law and most revered companion, ruled for two years. Initially the succession was in doubt. However, due to Abu Bakr's long-observed maturity and his immediate, wise move to step forward on the day of the Prophet's death, diverse elements of the community soon endorsed his leadership.

At the time of Muhammad's death, many of the independent Bedouin groups considered their loyalty to be with Muhammad personally. Through some twenty-three military strikes, Abu Bakr's forces subdued the Bedouins and brought them back into the umma.

Umar ibn al-Khattab, the Second Caliph, 634-644 CE

When Abu Bakr died, the question of succession was again problematic, but the Rashidun leadership chose Muhammad's son-in-law Umar over Ali, another son-in law. Thanks to Abu Bakr's effectiveness, Umar inherited a stable and loyal citizenry. Bedouin men proved to be excellent soldiers, and under Khalid b al-Walid, they became a formidable army. After several successful campaigns, the army captured Jerusalem and went on to defeat the Persian Empire.

During this period, Umar established a formal plan for dealing with the non-Muslim citizens of the empire, who in many areas remained in the majority for centuries. The plan, known as the Pact of Umar, mirrored in many respects the relationships established with subjected people in future generations. The people were guaranteed freedom of religion, and their persons and property were safe, but they were required to pay a special tax and their freedom was limited in several specific ways. For instance, they were prohibited from improving their places of worship and were not allowed to express their faith beyond the limits of their own homes and religious institutions.

In 644 CE, a Persian prisoner of war assassinated Umar, using a poisoned spear that caused a slow and painful death. Before dying, Umar appointed a six-man committee to choose his successor. Ali, who had lost out the last time, had hoped to become caliph, but he was passed over once again. This time he was deeply distressed, and his supporters were bitterly disillusioned. The choice was yet another son-in-law, Uthman ibn Affan. The result of this election was the beginning of a recognized Sunni/Shi'a division in the community. The Shi'a body, which favored Ali, had always believed the succession of leadership should be hereditary. The Sunni group was committed to a leadership selected by the inner council and based on demonstrated capability.

Uthman ibn Affan, the Third Caliph, 644-656 CE

Perhaps the most significant of Uthman's efforts was the collation of the Qur'an into a single, bound document. Tradition holds that at the time of Muhammad's death, there were fifteen men who had memorized the entire revelation that the Prophet had received. Uthman, in his authority as caliph, recognized that with the expanding Islamic domain, the revealed message must be carefully preserved and distributed for purposes of instruction. He directed Zayd ibn Thabit to gather all the revealed material and carefully prepare an official, parchment copy. Zayd had been Muhammad's chief secretary and was present when much of the later Surahs were received.

With the help of three men from Muhammad's tribe, Zayd gathered all the material and made a single copy. The four men then burned all varied copies, so from that time on, there was one recognized Arabic edition of the Qur'an. The four men then carefully made identical parchment copies that Uthman could give to trusted teachers and circulate throughout the realm.

As the Islamic community continued to expand into new and extended frontiers, Uthman appointed key leaders from among a group of his own relatives. Some of the family members Uthman had elevated to key positions of leadership betrayed his trust. They were accused of using community funds for their own enhancement. This undermined Uthman's authority, and he was accused of nepotism and mismanagement. After a twelve-year reign, Uthman was assassinated. Reputedly, a small contingent that had originally favored Ali was responsible for his death.

Ali ibn Abi Talib, the Fourth Caliph, 656-661 CE

Ali, now the last of the four close companions of the Prophet, was immediately recognized as the caliph. Those who had purportedly murdered Uthman were never apprehended, and Ali's leadership fell under a cloud of accusation that he was shielding the assassins. Uthman's relatives, joined by Aisha, Muhammad's favorite wife, formed a restive group in opposition to Ali. Aisha headed a military force that marched against Ali's camp in a misguided effort to remove him from power. Ali's forces quickly put down the revolt, which came to be known as the Battle of the Camel. Ali personally pardoned Aisha for her part in the rebellion and had her safely escorted back to Medina, where she was promised a lifetime allowance. Ali later moved the capital from Medina to Kufa.

Ali was credited with seeking to emphasize Muhammad's spiritual goals. After six years, however, Uthman's relatives were still disgruntled and antagonistic. In the midst of a subsequent battle, they requested a truce for negotiations. Ali granted their request, as required by the Qur'an, and a settlement was reached. Unfortunately, a subordinate group within Ali's own army was angered by the peace terms. Turning upon their leader, they murdered him. This ended the twenty-nine years of the Rashidun leadership.

The Umayyad Dynasty, 661–750 CE

The first dynastic line in Islamic history, the Umayyad dynasty, saw the breakdown of the Prophet's egalitarian ideal. Like Uthman, the Umayyad leadership tended to keep power within their own family hierarchy, as if they believed Islam was the property of the aristocracy. Their achievements were great as a sectarian force of kingdom builders but were lacking in the spiritual integrity that originally made Islam great.

A member of the Umayyad clan, Muawiyah I, moved into the power vacuum. Muawiyah I was the son of Abu Sufyan, Muhammad's one-time antagonist, and had already declared himself caliph in Damascus. Like his father, Muawiyah I was an accomplished leader. Moving the capital from Kufa to Damascus, he focused his energy on political competence and military expansion. His leadership style was open and even included Jews and members of the Christian community in key leadership positions. Sarjun, the son of the Christian mystic John of Damascus, was Muawiyah I's close advisor.

At Muawiyah I's death in 680 CE, the dynastic succession entered a period of crisis. In the five years from 680 to 685 CE, three Umayyad caliphs were recognized as leaders. As if that were not enough, two rival caliphs also claimed the right to rule. The most notable of the rivals was

Muhammad's grandson Husayn, the second son of Ali. Attempting to gain official recognition as caliph, Husayn left Mecca and marched with a small force toward Kufa, where his father Ali had been caliph. On the way, the forces of Muawiyah's son Yazid ambushed Husayn's caravan, in what is known as the Battle of Karbala, and Husayn was killed. Husayn was declared a martyr, and his death is observed at the Day of Ashura. It has become the key rallying point of Shi'a Islam and is a day of personal mourning. The Battle of Karbala and Husayn's death are perceived as the final point of division between the two Islamic groups and thus the distinctive point at which Shi'a Islam became an independent entity.

Finally, in 685 CE, Abdel-Malik, Abu Sufyan's great-grandson, gained full control of the growing Umayyad domain. He centralized the government and made Arabic the official language in all parts of the realm. Abdel-Malik introduced Muslim coinage, improving the economy of the regime.

People in new areas of Muslim conquest often welcomed the newcomers with eagerness, because Muslim expectations were typically more generous than those of earlier rulers. In keeping with this tradition, living conditions improved under Abdel-Malik's Muslim leadership. He furthered territorial expansion, including a military exploration into southern Spain. His crowning achievement, however, was the construction of the Dome of the Rock, the beautiful Muslim shrine on the Temple Mount and one of the main landmarks on the skyline of present-day Jerusalem.

In 717 CE, Caliph Umar ibn Abd al-Aziz began a short but notable reign. He unified the Muslim response to the vast ethnic variety of people who had come to live under the umbrella of Islam. People as divergent as Jews, Christians, Zoroastrians, and several polytheist groups were recognized under a common structure, as Muhammad had envisioned in his effort to achieve an egalitarian society. Umar ibn Abd al-Aziz was given the special honor as the only Umayyad caliph to be recognized in Islamic tradition as a genuinely religious caliph rather than a worldly king.

Following Umar, a number of military defeats ended geographic expansion. Notable among these defeats was the Battle of Tours in 732 CE, achieved by Charles Martel and the Franks, which ended Muslim expansion in western Europe. Other defeats occurred in the Far East at the door of Asia. Much of the problem at this point was simply the result of great early success. Vast numbers of highly diverse people produced the problems associated with assimilation. The expanded size of the empire, from Spain in the west to China and India in the east, resulted in a breakdown of communication, supply sources, and basic oversight and control. The once mighty Umayyad dynasty was on a slippery slope toward disintegration.

A Summary of and Reflection on the Umayyad Dynasty

The Umayyad period was notable for territorial expansion. Yet the failure to maintain equality among people, as Muhammad had sought, undermined the ethical integrity of the Prophet's vision. Some Muslim critics have gone so far as to indicate that the weakness of the Umayyad Dynasty was the result of the sinful failure of its leadership.

It is important to recognize that the difficulty of integrating political achievement and spiritual integrity has been a curse of governmental hubris from the time of King Solomon. It was this very concern that brought the pilgrims to Massachusetts, the Quakers to Pennsylvania, and the Roman Catholics to Maryland. Each sought to build a community where spiritual truth would be free of military pressure and political expediency. Yet the subsequent treatment of Native Americans, New England witches, African slaves, and Iraqi prisoners of war, among others, has cast a shadow across American history.

Neglect of the divine spirit and faulty use of power were dilemmas of the Umayyad Dynasty and the Middle Ages papacy, as well as Henry VIII and his newly created Church of England, which burned dissenters at the stake. Irrational immorality in others is a sin, but in ourselves can seem just a cultural accommodation to the circumstances of the time.

It was the attempt to correct this religious/political corruption that motivated the founding fathers of the United States to include the First Amendment to the Constitution, which stipulates, "Congress shall make no law respecting an establishment of religion, or prohibiting the free exercise thereof." This very concern still plagues both Islamic and Christian leadership. The fundamental question remains: How can we be faithful to God, build a strong community, and grant equal justice to all, while never allowing the misguided use of power and greed to destroy the values we cherish?

The Abbasid Dynasty, 750–1258 CE

In the midst of the disintegration of the Umayyad dynasty, the descendants of Muhammad's uncle Abbas came upon the scene. This previously unrecognized group of relatives established the powerful second dynasty, the Abbasids. In 747 CE, forces loyal to the Abbasid uprising assassinated some eighty leaders of the Umayyad house at a banquet. The new leadership, true to their method of achieving power by force, placed a leather carpet beside the caliph's throne to avoid soiling the fine woolen fabric of the Persian carpet when instant executions were performed.

The second caliph of the Abbasid dynasty, Caliph Harun al-Rashid, had the city of Baghdad built by one hundred thousand architects, craftsmen, and laborers in four years. He established cordial relations with Charlemagne of Europe. This relationship was partially based on the fact that the two leaders needed mutual support as each struggled with a powerful enemy. Charlemagne feared Byzantium, and Harun feared the remaining Umayyad leaders of Spain and North Africa. By 786 CE, Baghdad was the most significant city on earth, and the royal palace occupied half of it.

The passions of the early Abbasid leaders were knowledge and wisdom. Their efforts to acquire these qualities were not built primarily on their own creativity, but on the Greeks', as Arab historian Philip Hitti declares:

> At the time of the Arab conquest of the Fertile Crescent, the intellectual legacy of Greece was unquestionably the most precious treasure at hand. (The Greeks had gained much of it from Egypt, the Phoenicians, and the Hebrews.) Hellenism consequently became the most vital of all foreign influences in Arab life.[3]

The zealous quest for Greek as well as Indian wisdom was achieved most effectively by Caliph al-Ma'mun. In 830 CE, when the dynasty was secure and the new city built, he brought together in Baghdad the intellectual creativity of international geniuses to establish his Bayt al-Hikmah (House of Wisdom). The intellectual environment that he created, known as the Golden Age, and perhaps the first great university, were the crowning achievements of all Muslim intellectual creativity. The lasting influence of the university and its library made it a greater accomplishment than his predecessor's architectural triumph in building the fabled city of Baghdad.

What al-Ma'mun achieved was based on the work of a large translation team, coupled with an international academy of scholars. Tradition tells us that the person most responsible for this incredible intellectual activity was Hunayn ibn Ishaq, a man notable both for scholarship and character. He was a Nestorian Christian from al-Hirah, trained by a medical practitioner. Hunayn presided over the group of translators, most of whom were, by birth, Aramaic-speaking. (Aramaic was the vernacular in Palestine at the time of Jesus.) They translated from Greek to Aramaic and then into Arabic. The results of their efforts included the Greek works of Hippocrates, Dioscorides, Plato, and Aristotle, and the scientific works of Galen, as well as the Old Testament, translated from the Greek Septuagint into Arabic.

Hitti tells us that Caliph al Mutawakkil also appointed Hunayn as his personal physician. The caliph imprisoned Hunayn for a year for refusing to prepare a poison the caliph wished to use against an enemy. When brought to the caliph and threatened with death for his refusal, Hunayn said, "I have skill only in what is beneficial, and I have studied naught else."

Interestingly, the caliph then claimed that he was only testing Hunayn's integrity as a physician. Then the caliph asked Hunayn his real reason for refusing to prepare the poison. The great man is reported to have answered,

> Two things: my religion and my profession. My religion decrees that since we should do good even to our enemies, how much more to our friends. My profession is instituted for the benefit of humanity and limited to their relief and cure.[4]

In the late eighth century, an Indian traveler brought to the House of Wisdom two gems of Indian scholarship. One was a document on astrology that was later used to integrate the Greek and Indian systems of astronomy. The other was the use of the numerals we now call Arabic, which at this point first entered the Muslim collection of scientific wealth, followed later by the decimal system.

These treasures became an incalculable gift to human knowledge and were preserved in Arabic translation while Europe was passing through the Dark Ages. By the time of the European Renaissance, many of the original documents had been lost, and their Arabic translation saved them for posterity.

Before the time of Muhammad, Arabic was a language of lyric poetry perfected by the Bedouins. As noted previously, one reason Arab mothers placed their babies with Bedouin wet nurses was so the children might master the beauty of this poetic language. To the Bedouin poetry, Muhammad added the gift of Abraham's religious inspiration. Then, in the late eighth century, the wisdom of Greek and Indian philosophy was also made available to future scholars in the Arabic tongue. As Hitti humorously comments, "All this took place while Europe was almost totally ignorant of Greek thought and science. For while al-Rashid and al-Mamun were delving into Greek and Persian philosophy, their contemporaries in the West, Charlemagne and his lords, were reportedly dabbling in the art of writing their name."[5]

Hospitals were built in both Baghdad and Cairo during the Abbasid Dynasty. Physicians paid attention to public health, even visiting jails and setting up clinics in rural communities.

The Abbasidian leadership achieved all of this two hundred years before the first European university in Bologna, Italy. Their library surpassed all others in the advance of human knowledge of mathematics, astronomy, medicine, architecture, and general science, reaching its peak by the tenth century. The glory of the Abbasid Dynasty began to deteriorate through yet another civil war. However, the final downfall of Baghdad and its empire came with military destruction by the Mongols in 1258. The Abbasidians never regained their leadership following that tragic Mongol devastation.

Summary of the Abbasid Period of Splendor

During the Umayyad Period, Muslim influence became multiethnic and then expanded during the Abbasid Period to include the cultural and intellectual treasures of previous ages. As a result of this ethnic, cultural, and intellectual expansion, a new definition of the term

"Arab" developed around language and culture rather than national background.

The vast knowledge gathered at the House of Wisdom came from a broad intercultural background, representing cultures as diverse as Hebrew, Greek, Indian, Persian, Roman, Chinese, Christian, and Muslim. By the late ninth century, the Abbasids had translated great bodies of knowledge into Arabic. Although collected, nurtured, and established originally in Baghdad, this vast body of literature and knowledge was a reflection of the cosmopolitan and multiethnic resources of the far-flung Islamic empire. This merging of intercultural wisdom was also exemplified in the diverse architecture of many early mosques and churches.

The Qur'an and the prophetic traditions of the Hadith appear to share spiritual and philosophical truth with the Talmud, classical Greek philosophy, Roman law, and the literature of the Old and New Testaments. For example, the first Arab treatise on medicine, according to Hitti, was originally a Hebrew translation of a Greek tract written by a priest in Alexandria. This preservation of knowledge by the Abbasid dynasty at the House of Wisdom was later spread abroad and influenced culture and society across time and geography.

The Umayyad Dynasty at Cordova, 750-1492 CE

The only significant colonization effort by the Abbasid dynasty was the invasion of the Iberian Peninsula (present-day Spain and Portugal). The initial development of a new Muslim presence there soon resulted in political reprisal from an Umayyad prince who had escaped the Abbasid massacre in 747 CE. Prince Abd al-Rahman had successfully fled Damascus and joined the Berbers in Africa. There he gathered a military force, crossed the Mediterranean into Spain, and set up a second Umayyad dynasty in Cordova.

The Cordova government's policy, adopted from the Qur'an, gave religious freedom to Jews and Christians, yet kept them in a relatively second-class status by requiring the payment of a special fee and submission to Muslim authority. Nevertheless, the united effort of the Jews, Christians, and Muslims produced a thriving economic power that was a creative blend of advanced agriculture, crafts, and international trade. The second Umayyad dynasty created a currency-based economy, and Cordovan gold coins became a stable currency across Western Europe. By the tenth century, the population of Cordova had reached one hundred thousand.

Education was encouraged, and scholars assembled an immense library of thousands of books. This in large part was possible due to the earlier achievements of the former House of Wisdom in Baghdad. The arts and sciences flourished. Evidence of this flourishing can be seen today when one visits Spain's beautiful Muslim-built cities, Cordova, Seville, and Granada. Moving out from their center of power in Cordova, this second Umayyad dynasty built one of the most advanced civilizations in Europe during their seven centuries of Islamic influence.

A Current Reflection on the Islamic Civilization of Spain

Some claim that the West destroyed the creative Muslim kingdom in Spain. A careful look at the actual history tells a different story. The destruction of this great interracial, interreligious, national power was largely the result of dissident Muslim elements fighting each other.[6] Internal fragmentation resulted in a loss of power and political unity. Only under these weakened conditions was the newly united Spanish monarchy of Ferdinand and Isabella in a position to diminish Muslim influence and ultimately drive the Islamic garrison out of their last stronghold in Granada in 1492. The monarchs generously allowed the Muslim nobility to flee to North Africa. The beauty and creativity left behind still survive today.

The present bishops of Spain are now alarmed by the ambitious plans of Islamic leadership, who are again asserting their influence. As plans proceed for the building of lavish mosques near Cordova, Seville, and Granada, the bishops fear that, in the light of the Spanish fertility rate of 1.1, which is the lowest in Europe, the waning influence of the Roman Catholic Church, and immigration from the Middle East, the Christian faith will once again be eclipsed by Islam. They report that this advance into their country is being financed from abroad by the oil-rich countries of the Middle East and that Muslim leadership is drawn to Spain by the romantic nostalgia of the lost paradise of their Andalusian kingdom, when caliphs ruled much of Spain from the eighth to the fifteenth century.

The Fatimid Dynasty, 909-1171 CE

The third great dynasty of Islam in the Middle East was known as the Fatimid Dynasty. The founder of the dynasty, Abdullah al Mahadi Billah, was a descendant of Muhammad's daughter Fatimah and Ali ibn Abi Talib, the fourth caliph. This was the only dynastic group within Shi'a Islam. They were recognized for a period by all of Islam as the holders of the authority of the true caliph.

The dynasty had its origin in Ifriqiya, North Africa, a part of modern Tunisia. After conquering Egypt, they relocated their capital to Cairo. Under the Fatimid leadership, Egypt flourished. They developed an extensive trade network in both the Mediterranean Sea and the Indian Ocean, establishing trade and diplomatic ties all the way to China. In their time of strength, the Fatimid dynasty controlled North Africa, Sicily, Palestine, Syria, Yemen, and Hejaz.

The Fatimid dynasty was noted for its inclusive nature. Leaders were selected on the basis of ability. At times, there were Sunni Muslims, Jews, and Christians in high leadership positions. The Fatimid rule gave full religious freedom to the people where it held power, including the Coptic Christian community, which had leadership in Cairo. At the present time, the Christian Church in Egypt is stable but struggling to maintain its independence.

The Crusades–Power and Religion in Disarray: 1096-1218

The Crusades critically destabilized much of Europe, the Middle East, and North Africa for over one hundred years. Ostensibly, these series of wars were an effort by the Roman Catholic hierarchy to reclaim the city of Jerusalem and the surrounding area that had been the homeland of Jesus. Initially, therefore, the Crusades had strong spiritual and emotional appeal for the common people of Europe. In a broader sense, however, they were a political, military means intended by Rome to stop the advance of Islam and restore Rome's dominant influence over the eastern branch of Christendom.

In commissioning the First Crusade, the Church offered two startling benefits to those who signed on as crusaders. The first was a get-out-of-jail-free card to anyone who was in trouble with the law. Prison cells emptied, and about sixty thousand of the least promising citizens of Western Europe flocked to the call of the cross. The second benefit had eternal significance: a full dispensation of forgiveness for sin.

This huge ragtag army got no farther than Eastern Europe when they encountered the Paulican Arians. This group was an early form of radical Protestants whose rash theological rebellion threatened the authority of both Rome and the Eastern Orthodox branches of Christendom. Crusader zeal eagerly vented itself on the Paulicans, since their view of Jesus appeared to mimic the Muslim view. Both groups believed in the virgin birth of Jesus, the immaculate conception of Mary, and the work of the Holy Spirit; however they considered neither Jesus nor the Holy Spirit divine in nature.

Since the crusaders had engaged the Paulicans on their home turf, the Paulicans took full use of their advantage and succeeded in killing two-thirds of the vast army. The remaining twenty thousand Holy Land liberators fled. Only with the help of the emperor of Constantinople was the crusader army able to regroup and move on eastward, toward its original quest, the freedom of Jerusalem. This was no doubt a kindness the emperor came to regret, because when Godfrey's European army arrived to reinforce the crusaders, its first military action was to turn and attack Constantinople.

After a tedious march around the eastern end of the Mediterranean Sea through Syria, the crusaders reached their destination. Under Godfrey's leadership, this sad army, having escaped the penalties of sin and prison, now laid siege to the holy city of Jerusalem. They slaughtered Jews and Arabs, indiscriminately killing Christians and Muslims alike to conquer Jerusalem in 1099. Rather than returning the city to its former ecclesiastical rule under Rome, Godfrey arranged to have himself crowned King of Jerusalem.

Europe sent more soldiers in a second Crusade to reinforce the Jerusalem garrison in 1147. Nevertheless, Saladin and his strong Muslim force overwhelmed the Holy City with little bloodshed in 1187. The third Crusade, led by none other than King Richard of England, proved a tragic failure. Ravaged by battle and shipwreck, his forces returned to England in 1192.

The fourth Crusade set out from Europe to reclaim Jerusalem in 1203. It was perhaps the most notable for its folly and destruction. Upon reaching Constantinople, the capital of the Eastern Orthodox Church, the crusaders settled on an easier target than Jerusalem. Although Constantinople was the capital of a Christian domain, it was not part of the Roman Church. The crusader army succeeded in breaching the walls of Constantinople, perhaps the wealthiest city on earth. In a tragic rampage of destruction, the Crusaders mindlessly looted Hagia Sophia, the magnificent cathedral of Theodosius. They raided the Royal Palace, the stately mansion of the patriarch of the Eastern Orthodox Church, and many Constantinople churches. In the plunder, they carried away priceless relics, icons, and treasures that later came to adorn the churches and homes of Western Europe.

By the time of the fifth Crusade in 1218, the perceived goals of the Church were so varied that the given mandate was unclear. Eager clerics exhorted the fighters to attack the Muslims in Sicily and North Africa, as well as the Muslims of Turkey, Palestine, and Spain. Beyond all of this, they were also to attack the radically reforming Paulicans who had been joined by the Poor Men of Lyons, a later addition to the ranks of the emerging Christian Reformation.

Due to the varied pressures of confusing goals and an overwhelmed leadership, the fifth Crusade totally failed. Other crusades followed with insignificant effect on world history, other than to further weaken Europe by large capital investment in the war machine and a mounting contagion from the diseases returning crusaders introduced to their communities back home. Jerusalem continued as an ethically and religiously diverse city of Muslims, Jews, and Christians living in peace under Muslim rule until 1920, when it came under British mandate following World War I.

The one hundred years of crusader activity reveal an episode in Christian history that is now commonly seen as an awkward embarrassment. Church leadership appeared ruthless and greedy, while the people of the land making up the ranks of the crusaders seemed more like rowdy youth seeking high adventure than serious soldiers of Christ serving God and country. Today in the West, however, the term "crusader" generally connotes a person of noble courage devoted to a holy purpose. In the East, the view of the same group is one of ruthless marauders out to pillage and lay waste.

In the thirteenth century, both the Islamic Empire and the Holy Roman Empire suffered problems of internal stress and ineffective leadership. Each system was undermined by a focus on internal politics and a neglect of the fundamental spiritual needs of its people. The crusaders played a discordant note in a drama of religion gone astray.

The Ottoman Empire, 1299-1922

The Great Ottoman Empire began with an unpretentious fiefdom on the edge of the Turkish Byzantine frontier. Osman, an equally unpretentious young Muslim, served as its founding leader. Perhaps his advance into history occurred through a fortunate marriage. Osman's father-in-law had connections, and Osman's wife apparently had aspirations for upward mobility. By the time of Osman's death in 1326, he and his capable son Orhan had enlarged their territory to include several villages and a few towns west of the Sea of Marmara.

Orhan's crowning military achievement was the conquest of the significant city of Brusa, which ultimately surrendered after a long siege. Once Brusa was in Muslim hands, talented leaders from distant communities, seeing opportunities on a new frontier, joined forces with Orhan to provide leadership in this new Muslim community. Brusa was soon a center of Muslim education and commerce.

Following Osman's death, Orhan moved out in expanding circles of military and political occupation. He conquered Nicea in 1331 and Nicomedia in 1337, while Pergama and other towns of the area soon joined the sphere of Muslim influence.[7] The remaining years of the fourteenth century were strongly influenced by the effects of the plague known as the Black Death. Taking advantage of this period of fear and confusion in southeastern Europe, Orhan's younger son, Murad I, moved west into Europe. Murad's growing military forces overran a significant portion of the Balkans, including Bulgaria, Macedonia, and parts of Serbia. Murad died in 1389 while taking part in the victorious Battle of Kosovo.

A Local Principality Becomes an Acknowledged Nation

Upon his father's death on the Kosovo battlefield, Murad's older son, Bayezid, accepted responsibility for Ottoman leadership. Within two generations, the Ottoman Empire had grown from a petty fiefdom to a dominant power, stretching from the Danube River to the Taurus Mountains.[8]

Clouding Bayezid's ascension to power, however, was a sibling rivalry. His brother Yakub had also been a valiant warrior on the battlefield of Kosovo. Although young, he had already served his father well in several government positions, and Bayezid considered him a threat. So to consolidate his own power, Bayezid strangled Yakub. This action, an incredible violation of acknowledged Muslim morality, was the initial step in the ultimate moral disintegration of the Ottoman Empire.

Key to Ottoman success on the battlefield was the training of captured boys and youth. They were nominally converted to Islam, well equipped, schooled, and trained as an elite military body. These youths developed a bonded commitment to each other and to the Ottoman cause. They were known as *Janissaries*, and their skill and discipline earned them a fearsome reputation among all who opposed them in Europe.

Another interesting factor in the Ottoman advance was the open acceptance among its leadership of diverse cultures, ethnicities, and religions. In harmony with the Prophet Muhammad's egalitarian spirit, the advancing forces quickly adjusted and integrated with local societies. History notes a growing number of Greek, Albanian, and Serbian-speaking Muslims in the Balkan area of Eastern Europe as early as the fourteenth century.

As Islam spread from North Africa and the Middle East into Europe, the intermixing of Jews, Christians, and Muslims seemed to indicate a spirit of unity. Since the three faiths had developed from a common monotheistic base and shared a similar ethical understanding, some believed that unification could be easily achieved. Following the battle of Kosovo, the conditions of peace called for Bayezi to marry Despina, a Christian Serbian princess. Acknowledging their Muslim/Christian marriage, the couple named their sons Musa (Moses), Isa (Jesus), Mehmed (Muhammad), Suleiman (Solomon), and Kasimir (a Balkan Christian name). The interfaith marriage created a public display of interest in religious unification.

In 1402, Bayezid received a letter from Timur Leng, the Mongolian Turkoman chieftain who enjoyed a growing Middle Eastern influence. The letter warned Bayezid to pull back from his threatening military intrusion beyond the Euphrates River. Pointedly ignoring the warning, Bayezid neither withdrew his forces nor prepared for Timur's threatened military response. Unfortunately for Bayezid, Timur's words had not been an idle threat. Timur attacked with sudden fury and routed the Ottoman forces. Bayezid was taken captive and died a few weeks later in humiliation, with no plan in place for his successor.

Bayezid's four dominant sons, Suleiman, Musa, Isa, and Mehmed, were each assigned a portion of the kingdom, and over the next ten years they fought over the right to the sultan's title. At the end of a costly Ottoman civil war, only Mehmed remained, and in 1412 he was acknowledged sultan of the united Ottoman domain.

Mehmed turned out to be a highly competent leader. He recognized the tragic folly of the war, the wastefulness of the lavish court, and the moral weakness of his father's large harem. In great measure, he returned to the simple modest life of his great-grandfather and gained the deep loyalty of his people. After a ten-year reign generally marked by peace and unity, he died of a stroke.

Mehmed's son, Murad II, assumed the throne at the age of seventeen and also proved to be an effective leader, promoting unity and developing a highly effective education program for his sons and other promising youths of the domain. There was, however, one great psychological block remaining as a cloud over Ottoman power. The authority of Ottoman leadership extended in every direction from its hub in western Turkey. Yet, as if in mockery, the exalted Christian city of Constantinople stood out awkwardly in the midst of the Ottoman's success and power. The Eastern Orthodox Emperor occupied what would have appeared to be their rightful capital.

From Strength to International Dominance

Following the death of Murad II in 1451, his son Mehmed II took his place and assumed a role that was vastly different from his father's. He was well educated, spoke several languages, and had a broad understanding of philosophy and history. A highly self-disciplined man, Mehmed II responded to the rather haphazard administrative style of his father with a general reordering of the government and the military. With this complete, his first major undertaking was to challenge once and for all the psychological barrier at the center of his domain.

Mehmed II carefully organized a plan to capture Constantinople, the ancient centerpiece of the dying Byzantine Empire. Preparations lasted more than a year and involved analyzing every potential approach and every weak spot in the city's defenses. When the attack finally began in April 1453, some one hundred seventy thousand troops and three hundred ships had been mustered. Siege guns capable of launching huge cannonballs bombarded the city walls from land and sea. With a tremendous assault near the gate of St. Romanos, the city fell on May 29. For a full century, this city had been a defiant island of wealth, culture, and influence, and its falling created a sense of psychological satisfaction; from that day, Sultan Mehmed II was referred to as Fatik the Conqueror.

A second, significant benefit of Mehmed II's reign was the broad expansion of the palace school. The far-flung government was in great need of effective administrative leadership. To address this problem, children aged ten to fourteen were conscripted from across the empire, carefully screened, and given a demanding ten- to twelve-year education. The curriculum of the palace school included languages, philosophy, history, science, mathematics, military logistics, law, theology, physical fitness, manual training, and personal conduct.

Graduates of the palace school were expected to assume the affairs of state in various positions throughout the realm. Having come from all parts of the empire, they were suited by language and culture to return to their places of birth to give service to the nation that had so carefully equipped them. The quality of this cadre of leadership had much to do with the ongoing effectiveness of the nation over the next hundred years.

When Mehmed II concluded his reign in 1482, the Ottoman Empire was the most powerful military and intellectual force on earth. It was a nation with leadership in mathematics, astronomy, and the study of the Greek philosophers. These notable Western classics were again preserved in Arabic translation. The religion of the Prophet Muhammad was the dominant faith and a leading force in knowledge and culture.

The close of the fifteenth century, however, saw increasing Ottoman conflict with their various realms across the Middle East. Of special concern was a strong religious and political threat from Shah Ismail of Iran. Ismail claimed descent from the Prophet Muhammad, Ali, and the Shiite Seventh Imam. This Iranian leader assumed his throne in

1502 and declared the Shiite version of Islam to be the official doctrine of the realm.[9]

Nevertheless, for thirty years following Mehmed II's death, his son Bayezid II presided over a peaceful and tolerant kingdom. He was a temperate man with philosophical interests. He never attacked a neighboring domain unless strongly provoked. In a demonstration of strong Jewish/Muslim bonds, Bayezid II welcomed one hundred thousand Jews into his domain as they fled the wrath of the Spanish monarch Isabella and her Inquisition in 1492. Yet personally he was a strict and devout Sunni Muslim.[10]

After Bayezid II's death, a brutal succession unfolded over the Sunni/Shiite split. Before his father's death, the favored son Ahmed adopted the Shiite religious position to placate Ismail of Iran. Although seriously ill at the time, Bayezid II denounced Ahmed's decision and abdicated in favor of another son, Selim. Selim recognized the internal intrigue in his midst and moved against his brothers and nephews, killing them all.

In eight years, Selim changed the international scene in the Middle East. He denounced the Shiite influx into his kingdom from Iran and purged them. When further trouble developed with Iran and Egypt, Selim again took the offensive. He defeated Shah Ismail in response to the Shah's religious interference in Ottoman affairs. When the Mamluk sultan of Egypt marched across the Ottoman borders into Syria in 1516, Selim again took the offensive, and Egypt fell to the Ottoman nation.

Selim's success was largely a matter of weaponry. While the Ottomans were equipped with muskets and artillery, their hapless enemies were still fighting with swords and arrows. In response to Selim's display of firepower, other communities decided to join his ranks. Aleppo, Damascus, Beirut, and other Middle Eastern cities opened their gates and accepted Selim's leadership. As a result of this vast realignment of Middle Eastern power, Selim was confident to claim the authority of the Abbasid Caliph in Cairo, transferring his title and authority to the Ottoman sultan. This made him the heir of the medieval Umayyad and Abbasid empires and consolidated the Muslim world under a single sultan/caliph crown.

According to one historian, Selim's achievements were due to the fact that:

His tastes were simple, he read widely, slept little, and was disinterested in his harem. His passion was his nation and its people, the Ottoman Empire. For them he lived and did much to refocus and solidify their dominant place in international affairs.[11]

Selim's father had prepared the way with beloved and loyal subjects and a highly trained, efficient administration. Bayezid II and Selim left Selim's son Suleiman all the ingredients necessary to establish the grand Ottoman Empire as the dominant international power. For the next forty-six years, Suleiman ruled a larger area for a longer time than any other leader in human history, earning him the name Suleiman the Magnificent. In Suleiman's domain, conquered peoples were free to follow their own religion and qualified men among them were eagerly accepted as participants in local and national government. However, while Suleiman's reign began in triumph, after four and a half decades it entered a period of decline.

The Sad Spectacle of Decline and Decay

While Europe developed, the Ottoman Empire began to stagnate intellectually as later leadership focused primarily on holding together its vast and diverse groups. Where formerly the ruler encouraged intellectual aspiration, following Suleiman the palace leadership in Constantinople (Istanbul) appeared to slowly refocus its energy on empire maintenance and internal intrigue. The large royal court surrounded itself in luxury unimagined by its spiritual founder, the Prophet Muhammad.

Signs of this weakening change could be seen in many painful specifics. For instance, upon coming to the throne in 1574, Murad III considered it expedient to murder his five younger brothers to safeguard his power. The sultan's reputation for murdering members of the royal family clearly undermined basic morality. Arrangements were even made for future sultans to have brothers caged in the palace complex so there would be no competition for the throne.

By the nineteenth century, the Ottoman government, once comprised of the military and scientific leaders of the world, was hiring German officers to train their army and Sir Douglas Gamble of England to strengthen their navy. A lavish lifestyle at the court and little attention to the political affairs of the empire had taken its toll. The royal leadership no longer led but spent its days in idleness or entertainment. Grand viziers were in charge of the affairs of state. On occasion, the mother of the sultan or his favorite lady might control affairs from behind the scenes. The sultan was only called upon to make key decisions, such as the disastrous step taken by Muhammad VI in 1914, when he decided to join Germany in World War I, effectively sealing the fate of the last Islamic world power.

The Final Conflict

At the outset of the twentieth century, the once-mighty Ottoman Empire, still vast in geographical scope, had become a dependent, second-rate power. In 1918, as their Axis partner Germany fell before the Allies, the weakness of Ottoman moral leadership became fully apparent. Muhammad VI deserted, as his people struggled to salvage the national integrity of Turkey. He made a private offer to the British to allow them to enter the capital in exchange for his personal safety. Leaders loyal to the integrity of the nation moved the government to Ankara, while the compromised sultan led a faltering sham government until 1922, when he left Istanbul on a British warship.

On October 30, 1918, the Allies and the newly formed Turkish government of Ankara signed the Armistice of Mudros on a British warship. What had been the Ottoman Empire was vastly reduced by Russian victories in the east and British and French cooperation with Arab nationalists in Syria, Palestine, and North Africa. At the Treaty of Versailles, when the western European nations carved up their trophies of victory, nothing was left of the Ottoman Empire's sweeping trans-Mediterranean possessions. The result was a political redistribution of the Middle East, dictated by France and England. In that settlement, the nation of Iraq was created from three eastern provinces of Anatolia.

Following the Armistice of Mudros, the Ankara government thought the calamity was over. But suddenly the Allies, divided in their goals, challenged the settlement recently reached at the Mudros accord. On May 15, 1919, backed by British, French, and US ships, a large Greek force landed at the Turkish port of Smyrna. The Greek invasion began with a massacre of Muslim citizens in the integrated Christian-Muslim city. Then the Greeks moved east into Turkey to the point agreed upon by their Allied protectors. In January of 1921, however, the Greek forces made a further, unauthorized advance into the heart of Turkey.

Responding to this unilateral move, the Allies deserted Greece within a month, declaring neutrality in the long-ranging Turkish/Greek rivalry. On August 26, six days after the declaration of Allied neutrality, the Turks began an offensive to regain their lost land. At great cost of life and property, the desperate Turkish army drove the Greek invaders back. With a slash-and-burn policy, the Greek army retreated to the coast, leaving nearly a million Muslims and Christians homeless. Boarding ships in Smyrna, the Greeks left the Christian Greek population there to face the condemnation of the bitter Turkish Muslim community that had been senselessly ravaged by the earlier Greek invasion.

On October 13, 1922, the Ankara government, along with Greek and Allied representatives, drew up an armistice that later became the basis of the Treaty of Lausanne. This was the final treaty of World War I, signed on July 14, 1923. It acknowledged the sovereignty of Turkey as we know it today.

Under the unifying leadership of Turkish general Mustafa Kemal, known in the West as Kemal Ataturk, the divided sections of the government were joined. The position of sultan was abolished, as the government officially became a republic and permanently moved from Istanbul to Ankara. The spiritual position of caliph was briefly retained, and then in 1924 it was also vacated, remaining so to the present. The great nation that had held the spiritual authority of caliph and the power lodged in the sultan for seven centuries was reduced to humiliation and war-torn poverty. This history doubtless played a role in inspiring the acts of terror of September 11, 2001.

Summary and Reflection

As we review Islamic history from the seventh century through the early twentieth century, we see a focus on Islamic military dominance and intellectual achievement. In the tenth century, there were three Islamic centers of power: a declining Abbasid base in Damascus, the Fatimid Dynasty centered in Cairo, and the second Umayyad Dynasty with its government in Cordova, Spain. There had been some two hundred years of unified authority. Then the tension of political struggle within the dynastic groups and between the Sunni and Shiite visions of Islam resulted in a significant decrease in Islamic cohesive power and prestige.

The weakness was compensated for by the emergence of the Ottoman Empire. This mighty collection of ethnic centers under a common political and religious entity was highly successful for a time. As long as the leadership was competent, the political realm was strong. But political advance and territorial gain was made at the expense of spiritual vitality. With ultimate power at the top, the two international power brokers of the Middle Ages—the Ottoman Empire and Catholic Christendom—displayed despotism and internal spiritual weakness.

As we reflect on this sweep of Islamic history, we see periods of notable achievement, such as the intellectual mastery gathered by the House of Wisdom of the Abbasid Dynasty and the vibrant cultural and economic achievement of the integrated second Umayyad Dynasty centered in Cordova, Spain. These periods demonstrate occasions of great pride in outstanding achievement. They illustrate the vibrant moral, cultural, intellectual, and spiritual potential found in the inspiration of Islam. Other periods demonstrate the internal contradiction of Islamic history, when the Prophet's vision and spiritual message were ignored and internal greed or corruption reduced competing Islamic factions to warring, self-destructive annihilation.

As we look at this history, we see interesting similarities between Christian and Muslim religious values. Each has achieved much in advancing human welfare, yet both have an amazing inclination to give lip service to a set of wonderful virtues while consistently ignoring their practical application. Before offering critiques of one another, each should embrace what they claim to believe while expressing grace and forbearance toward the other. The vibrant moral vision of Jesus and Muhammad offers the people of the earth the possibility of peace and justice. This book seeks to motivate Christians who struggle with God's call to be peacemakers in the midst of global uncertainty.

Chapter 10

The Motivations Stirring the Terrorists

The tragic record of radical violence since 1970 prompts us to ask, "What sparked this outpouring of crime in the skies, on the sea, and in the streets?" Research offers no accurate, unbiased answer to that question. The complexity of the present crisis is best viewed in the context of the interwoven strands of history from the tenth through the twentieth century. An amazing amount of foul play unfolded across time. The Crusades and the Inquisition are but two tragedies in a long litany of destructive history. Christians as well as Muslims have played a significant role in the record of crimes against humanity committed in the name of religion.

Historical issues in the last hundred years clarify the critical differences between those who follow the true Islamic faith and those who commit terror in the name of Islam. The ability to distinguish clearly between a terrorist regime and a faithful Muslim community is fundamental to the purpose of this book. The information covered in this chapter equips us to make this distinction.

Terrorism in the name of Islam emerges out of two distinct issues, and each is an aspect of motivation. The first issue is ideology or worldview.[1] The second issue is best understood as "the offending event," the action of others perceived as an affront to the honor or economic well-being of Muslim people. Understanding each of these issues allows us to gain a clear awareness of the dynamics that trigger international unrest and terrorism.

Hate ideology is one of the consistent ingredients in distorted Islamic terrorism. After 9/11, Americans often raised the question, "Why do they hate us?" Part of the answer is that history, especially events of the last century, has taught Muslims to hate us. The second half of this chapter pursues that aspect. But first we need to seek an answer to the question, "What is the ideological structure of terrorism—the deliberately distorted view of Islam—that produces hate and destructive actions?" It is critically important that we understand the answer. It can be our guide in wisely confronting radical terrorism.

The First Motivation: The Ideology of Purist or Radical Islam

The Qur'an, in accordance with all monotheistic teaching, puts a primary focus on God and on each individual's relationship with God. Out of this focus comes love for God and love for neighbor, personal virtue, and communal peace. The radicals, however, have reverted to their ancient Bedouin tribal roots, where the focus is on divine demands and the honor of tribal group loyalty. They believe this will give them the means to regain control of their history and end their perception that the West is encroaching on their power.

The focus of the radicals is on rigid expectations. Rather than reflecting the teaching of the Qur'an, these expectations emphasize the culture of the national group. We can see this clearly in the Taliban. Instead of centering on the egalitarian oneness of all humanity under the compassionate care of God, the Taliban's morality is distorted by ancient tribal rules, symbolically exemplified by the total covering of a woman from head to toe when she is in a public place. Islam teaches modesty, but certainly does not imply that women are impure unless they keep their bodies totally hidden from view. The radical goal is not to safeguard the teaching of the Prophet but to promote the pre-modern dominance of a rigid, paternalist culture.

Another result of this distorted ideology is the terrorist strategy of suicide bombing. First, note that suicide is a mortal sin for a Muslim (Surah 4:29–30). Rather than seventy virgins, hell is the reward. Second, Muhammad taught that in battle it is forbidden to kill non-combatants, especially women and children, as so often happens in suicide bombings. In this one issue—suicide bombing—we have a vivid illustration of two basic ideological differences separating true Islam from the terrorists' worldview. Understanding these distinctions is crucial if we are to recognize the deep divide between Islam and the ideology of hate.

The Jurists, an Early Voice of Stability

Radicals pose a challenge to maintaining the spiritual purity and practice of any faith. In Islam, this concern focuses on the original message given by the Prophet Muhammad and how that message is to be interpreted in the modern age. For centuries, this interpretive work was the responsibility of jurists, scholars fully trained in Islamic theology and law. These jurists mediated the various reactions to change and maintained stability.

Initially, jurists were widely respected for their classical knowledge of the Qur'an and the *Sunna* or *Hadith* (the prophetic tradition). Over the centuries, their work involved an ongoing interpretive process resulting in the accumulation of the Shari'ah (Islamic law), which has come to include some fifty thousand titles, several of which are many volumes long.[2] The authority of the jurists in Islam was somewhat like the role of the Papal Curia in Rome. Their method of functioning, however, was less dogmatic and provided guidance for both theology and practical legal policy. Their significance is seen in the following description of the Shari'ah, which includes both specific laws and principles of law:

> The Shari'ah is God's justice among His servants, and His mercy among His creatures. It is God's shadow on this earth. It is His wisdom which leads to Him in the most exact way and the most exact affirmation of the truthfulness of His Prophet. It is His light which enlightens the seekers and His guidance for the rightly guided.[3]

From the ninth century to the eighteenth century, Muslims depended on the authority of the jurists to determine the structure of religious doctrine and practice. The collection of the multi-layered Shari'ah was the bonding element that gave worldwide Islam its unity across not only nine centuries of time, but also across the various political divisions and governmental structures in the changing landscape of the Islamic world.

The vast compendium of religious law was the glue that gave the Islamic world its sense of unity.

The defining role of the jurists and their extensive collection of Islamic jurisprudence, or Shari'ah, started to lose its uniting authority at the beginning of Western colonialism. The initial intruders into the domain of Islam were the forces of Napoleon with their entrance into North Africa in the eighteenth century.

In the turmoil of a weakening Ottoman Empire, the respect traditionally given to the jurist class disintegrated. Gifted Muslim students turned to the West for legal training. Those who did become Islamic jurists lost status in their own society. Over time, the mediating authority of Shari'ah was severely compromised under the guise of modernity and reform as well as a shifting tide of Western legal and social influence.

The vacuum created by the lack of a strong Islamic jurist authority awakened a need for renewed purity, which in turn opened the door for radical reformers. In Egypt, the Salafi ("earlier one" or "original") movement, especially evidenced in the Muslim Brotherhood, appears to have filled this authority vacuum. In Arabia, the Wahhabi group became the dominant reform voice.[4] Responding to the absence of a recognized Islamic court of appeals (the role of the jurists), both reform groups have expressed their frustration through violence.

An Illustration from the Present: Tragedy and Hope

Islam does not have an authoritative clergy as found in the hierarchies of many Christian denominations. Its structure is similar to the Quakers: open and democratic. This fact, coupled with the absence of a central modern jurist authority, helps explain the lack of a rapid and unified Muslim response as the world demanded answers concerning the Islamic stand on terror after 9/11. Individual Islamic groups posted repudiation of the terrorists' actions on their websites, and the governments of Middle Eastern nations expressed regret. But no recognized voice from Mecca, Cairo, Baghdad, or Tehran rebuked Osama bin Laden or emphatically clarified the Islamic position regarding this ultimate tragedy. UCLA Islamic scholar Khaled Abou El Fadl eloquently expresses the consternation of both the non-Muslim world and faithful followers of Islam when he writes:

It is not an exaggeration to say that in the minds of many in the world, Islam has become intimately associated with what can be described as ugliness—intolerance, persecution, oppression, and violence. Whether one believes this view of Islam and Muslims is justified or not, it has become an undeniable fact that in many parts of the world, the very word *Islam* arouses negative sentiments that range from suspicious indifference to fear or intense dislike. For a Muslim who cares about his or her faith, this reality arouses intense feelings of hurt and anguish. More than a billion people find in Islam their emotional and spiritual sustenance and fulfillment. For those Muslims, Islam is their source of serenity and spiritual peace, and Islam offers moral and ethical guidance that, instead of ugliness, fills their lives with beauty. How does a Muslim reconcile between the faith he or she lives and experiences and the prevalent public perceptions in the non-Muslim world?[5]

Then, in a note of hope, Abou El Fadl adds, "I will argue that indeed Islam is at the current time passing through a transformative moment no less dramatic than the Reformation movements that swept through Europe at one time and led to long and bloody religious wars."[6]

What we see is an acknowledged awareness by a noted Muslim scholar of a lack of clear guidance and interpretation within the Muslim community. Perhaps on the part of some there is a reticence to speak up forcefully, lest they find themselves isolated individuals, alone and ridiculed for betraying the faith when unity is needed. This illustrates the problem generated by the absence of the jurist's authoritative role that once guided the conscience of the Muslim world.

There appears to be a need to again balance interior jihad (the struggle to maintain personal moral and spiritual purity) with exterior jihad (the struggle to control social and political conditions). The essence of the Prophet Muhammad's achievement was his ability to keep the two in creative balance. Muhammad's goal was always clear: to build a strong and peaceful community submissive to the authority of God. From the evidence seen in Osama bin Laden's activity, the goal for his so-called jihad is the destruction of community.

When we tackle complex issues, such as the building of an Islamic community center and mosque near Ground Zero, it requires a delicate balancing act that respects the sensitivities of the victims of terrorism, the rights of Muslim citizens, and the values we hold dear as a nation. In the coming months and years, there will be many more such challenges requiring mature judgments that lead to sound public policy. How well we respond will determine the spiritual health of our communities and the long-term integrity of our nation.

The Ascendancy of Wahhabi Ideology

A new, militant interpretation of Islam appeared on the scene in the late eighteenth century. It originated when a radical by the name of Ibn Abd al-Wahhab[7] joined forces with an emerging Arabian leader, Ibn Al-Sa'ud, who has been described by both his admirers and detractors as a conniving desert chieftain. Abd al-Wahhab promoted a doctrine so radical and hateful that his own brother, Sulayman, condemned him as a danger to Islam.[8]

The Wahhabi policy for interpreting scripture was the reverse of the tested scholarly approach to the Qur'an. Wahhabists conformed to their own doctrinaire goals rather than base their actions on the teachings of the Qur'an. For instance, leaders of the radical movement used texts inspired during the Medina defense against the Mecca invasion out of context to justify a militant interpretation of overall Muslim practice. They totally ignored the Prophet's patient, peaceful approach to gaining the loyalty of Mecca.

Through this discredited use of the Qur'an, they claimed that hatred, cruelty, and torture were legitimate, even though the Qur'an specifically condemns such conduct. After gaining power in cooperation with Al-Sa'ud, the Wahhabi leaders killed and pillaged communities that in any way opposed their position. This teaching and conduct of the radical Wahhabi movement was in total violation of the life and teaching of Muhammad. The present-day actions of al Qaeda, rooted in the Wahhabi teachings, are not true Islam, but rather a perversion.

UCLA Islamic scholar El Fadl writes:

> The story of puritanical Islam should properly
> start with the Wahhabi.... It is unequivocal,
> however, that they have influenced every
> puritanical movement in the Muslim world
> in the contemporary age. Every single Islamic
> group that has achieved a degree of international
> infamy, such as the Taliban and al-Qa'ida, has
> been heavily influenced by Wahhabi thought.
> By discarding and at times demonizing the
> classical heritage and its interpretations, Abd al-
> Wahhab ... was able to reinject these precedents
> of cruelty into the heart of Muslim theology
> and law, thereby reinventing Islam on the basis
> of a new immorality.... Muslim extremists such
> as Bin Laden ... followed in the footsteps of
> Abd al-Wahhab by relying on the same exact
> precedents of cruelty as a means of justifying
> killing innocent people.[9]

Radical Wahhabi doctrines are frequently reported to the world as true Islamic teachings. Since their source is Saudi Arabia, the center of the holy sites of Islam, the unaware accept them as authentic Islamic doctrine. This makes the need for factual clarification all the more urgent. Non-Muslims are being influenced to distrust all Muslims, because they assume the hate literature from Saudi Arabia is authentic Muslim teaching.

The Wahhabi-Saudi alliance had always decided its course on the basis of political power. At the outset of World War I, they expanded their influence by accepting British aid. The terms of the agreement permitted them to further expand Wahhabi policy. As Stephen Schwartz, former editorial writer for the Voice of America, has written,

> To arrive at an understanding with the British,
> with the goal of transforming the umma into a
> community of Wahhabi fundamentalists, was
> a concept so daring in its perversity it would
> seem to have sprung from the brain of a demon,
> not a man.[10]... [Their success in implementing

> Wahhabi concepts under British auspices was so significant,] the Wahhabis interpreted [it] as a sign of God's favor[11] ... The British seem never to have thought that a "reformed" Islam, stripped of its customary culture and impregnated with separatism, supremacism, and violence in the name of virtue ... might someday launch a suicidal, destructive challenge to the Christian world.... Eventually, the Wahhabis interpreted the failure of the Western powers to perceive their intent as a sign of the unbelievers' stupidity.[12]

This initial lack of awareness continued as Wahhabi-Saudi Arabian deception was repeated in their dealings with the United States. The Wahhabi deception was also evident in the rise of the Arabian oil industry, the anti-Russian war in Afghanistan, and even the events after September 11, 2001. The Saudi state supplied the oil to thirsty American industry. Indirectly, through Wahhabi tradition, it also supplied the suicide doctrine that motivated Hamas (the self-appointed political protectors of Palestinian justice) and the Palestinian terrorist movement. And ultimately, Saudi Arabia, with its Wahhabi religious education preparation, was the home country of the pilots that perpetrated the terror of 9/11.

Thus we see the key role of a distorted, radicalized ideology. It is urgent we recognize that although this terrorist ideology is linked to Islam, it is distinctly different from true Islam in its teaching and its practice. Not to recognize this fundamental distinction leads to stigmatizing faithful United States citizens who are Muslims. Failure to clearly make this distinction also results in our failure to correctly identify our enemy and develop a wise, ideological strategy to neutralize and eventually disarm them.

Radical Ideology in Its Modern Application

September 11, 2001 was in a sense like December 7, 1941. For most of us who remember both days, Pearl Harbor was a long way away, unless you were a Navy mom. But the World Trade Center, the Pentagon, and the Pennsylvania field were either next door or then marked on our calendars and in our hearts. They are places that are part of our ego identity. Those three thousand people were our neighbors, our friends, our family. The planes that bombed Pearl Harbor were enemy planes bombing a military installation. The planes that wreaked havoc on 9/11 were our planes destroying our centers of life, planes piloted by a faceless, radical, terrorist enemy.

This enemy appears to hold an abiding hatred for us—for who we are and to that which we are committed. Their ideology is one for which they are willing to die. This is one of the chief reasons for our gnawing inner stress. "Why do they hate us?" many continue to ask. It is an ideological question we must answer if we are to achieve peace and address the mind and heart issues that lie behind terrorist actions.

How could those men live among us and still feel such deep hatred as they trained and learned to fly our planes? How could they offer their daily prayers to God, yet move toward such terrifying murder? How could they calmly face their own deaths when they had so many options for life? We are confused, we are angry, and we are afraid. There is far more to the 9/11 story than what happened in that carefully planned event on a beautiful fall morning in 2001.

The master of that diabolical scheme was at work in the planning for well over two years. He had struck several times before, and he solemnly promises to strike again. His name is Osama bin Laden. He is out there, planning still.

Bin Laden is a Sunni Muslim educated in Saudi Arabia under the influence of the Wahhabi cult. His initial passion appears to have been to drive the Russians from Afghanistan. There he honed his skills as a recruiter, trainer, and fighter. He initially financed his efforts out of his own personal wealth. The United States, Saudi Arabia, and other countries supplied additional financing for the battle against the Russians. His influence proved significant in battling the Russians in Afghanistan. Under his leadership, bin Laden's men prevailed. Many in the Middle East see him as a wealthy young man who left everything behind to follow God in a holy war—a hero.

Having prevailed against the Russians, bin Laden then turned his fury on America. Offended by the Saudi monarchy for welcoming American forces into the holy land where Mecca and Medina are located, bin Laden remained in Afghanistan, focusing on the recruitment and training of special forces to engage the West in an ongoing jihad. The continuing United States military involvement in the Middle East has fueled recruitment, and his forces, called al Qaeda, are reported to have operatives around the world.

Homegrown, radical terror cells connected to al Qaeda extended the group's reach even further. In each case, citizens of the country harmed were connected to a local terrorist cell and directly involved in the attack. The results of their efforts are seen in at least four countries of the European Union. In Holland and France, the occurrences were primarily street violence. In Spain and then in England, the violence focused on public transportation and resulted in loss of life as well as increased fear and uncertainty. Each of these situations has a local context, but they share a common ideological motivation.

The Second Motivation: Offending Events

> God has struck America at its Achilles heel and destroyed its greatest buildings, praise and blessings to Him. America has been filled with terror from north to south and from east to west, praise and blessings to God. What America is tasting today is but a fraction of what we have tasted for decades. For over eighty years our umma has endured this humiliation and contempt. Its sons have been killed, its blood has been shed, its holy sanctuaries have been violated, all in a manner contrary to that revealed by God, without anyone listening or responding.[13]

These are the opening lines of a dramatic message taped by Osama bin Laden and broadcast on the Arabic television network Al Jazeera in early October 2001. His words provide us with an effective link between the *ideology* and the *offending events* motivating terrorism. The actions of al Qaeda itself give shape to the ideology of terrorism. But to identify the offending events that motivate terrorism, we must explore what bin Laden meant when he referred to more than eighty years of humiliation and degradation. For that, it is instructive to recall the events that occurred at the end of World War I.

The once-mighty Islamic Empire was a tragic memory, having at one time extended west through Spain, southeast into India, and northeast beyond the Caspian and Black Seas. The nation that for seven centuries held the spiritual authority of the Muslim caliph and the secular power of the sultan was reduced to war-torn poverty, a fraction of its former size. The full flower of Islamic achievement in the largest and one of the longest-enduring nations in history fell before the firepower of France, England, and the United States.

At the peace conference of Versailles in 1919, the western Allied nations carved up their trophies of victory. Germany, the dominant aggressor in World War I, was stripped of its colonies but allowed to continue under its own government. The Arabs, on the other hand, were betrayed. The British ignored both its own citizen, the legendary Lawrence of Arabia, and the agreement that it had made with the Arabs at the outset of the war. The Muslim and Christian Arabs, originally part of the Ottoman Empire, who ironically had served as part of the Allies' defense, were dealt with as a conquered people.

The result was a political redistribution of the vast Ottoman Empire, including the present Middle East and North Africa. These lands were divided into colonial protectorates controlled by France and England. Even Muslims in the Far East came under a colonial government, the Royal Dutch East Indies. As one Muslim writer expressed, "In 1918 … every Muslim in the world lived under foreign subjugation, every single one!"[14]

The climax of World War I makes clear what is meant by an offending event. The dramatic change in the political fortunes of the Muslim people and the betrayal of the Arabs in the Versailles Peace Treaty are painful wounds stimulating long-term resentment. At the very point when the Wahhabi radical ideology was fully established in early twentieth-century Saudia Arabia, this tragic set of offending events fueled the fire for revenge.

In his statement, bin Laden offers us a unique opportunity to view the two manifestations that motivate him and the terror he promotes. As he thanks God for the great destruction he achieved on 9/11, bin Laden expresses the deep intensity of the distorted ideology of Wahhabi hate within himself. After all, he grew up where the Wahhabi dogma was the required religious standard in the educational system of Saudi Arabia.

Then, with poetic clarity, bin Laden documents the offending event resulting from the Versailles Treaty: Muslim humiliation at the hands of Western colonialism. He says, "What America is tasting now is something insignificant compared to what we have tasted for scores of years. Our nation has been tasting this humiliation and this degradation for more than eighty years." This, he believes, justifies the hate and terror of his revenge. It had been eighty-two years since the treaty's arbitrary division of the Islamic Ottoman Empire and the betrayal of the North African Arabs after World War I.

A proud people crushed seek revenge. Generally recognized as visionary people, many Muslims (like many Christians) are committed to the premise that God intends their faith to master the paganism of the world. Contrary to the actual teaching of the Prophet Muhammad, yet ideologically highly motivated, those who flew the planes on 9/11 died for the reality of their faith. Not with sympathy or approval, but with candid awareness, we must grasp the ideological motivation and the historical events that prompt radical terror if we are to be in a position to respond with understanding.

Three Points of Social Stress Dividing Islam and the West

In addition to historical offenses, Muslims cite three social stresses dividing Islam and the West. The first is the perceived moral disintegration in the West. Muslims see evidence for this in Western media mocking sexual morality and flaunting extravagance and greed in the face of international hunger and disease. Many Muslims claim that such entertainment is a basic denial of monotheistic morality. It is an offense to the moral concerns of Muslim family and communal life. Perhaps there are Christian and Jewish families who would concur.

The second social stress is over the charge that the United States vocally promotes democratic freedom but in practice backs governments led by autocratic leaders who promote US financial interests. Three illustrations are frequently mentioned. One is the 1953 CIA-led coup to reestablish the discredited Shah of Iran (virtually a US puppet), over Muhammad Mossadeq, a popular elected Iranian leader. Iranians believe this was done to benefit American business interests. A second illustration is the well-known complaint that the United States supported Saddam Hussein after he attacked Iran in the late 1970s, and western armament firms sold munitions to both sides. The third example is American diplomatic ties with Saudi Arabia, a source of significant petroleum and technical business exchange. Muslims consider this pattern of promoting business interests ahead of national moral and cultural commitments as ethical hypocrisy. Even the United States government acknowledges that the Saudi nation is the foremost supplier of Wahhabi hate literature.[15] Saudi Arabia is also considered a source of Wahhabi-trained imam leaders for schools and mosques around the world.

The third social stress relates to the stand of the Qur'an against usury, defined in Islamic law as the practice of loaning and borrowing funds at a standard rate of interest. Banking and corporate enterprise have been at the center of Western economic progress, while loans have historically been unavailable to Muslim business due to the Quranic disapproval of usury. Only recently has Islamic law been modified so that some forms of corporate business practice are legal under Islamic law.

A Critical Point of Division: Jewish/Palestinian Tension

For the last sixty years, the Palestinian situation has been the central offending event that has motivated the terrorists. The recognition of Israel in 1948 set the stage for the creation of the Palestinian Liberation Organization (PLO). Later expressions of Arab discontent led to the formation of Hamas. In the mind of the West, the ongoing conflict between the Palestinians and the Jews is the focus of the issue. Meanwhile, the history behind this tragic struggle remains virtually ignored. It is of no small consequence that for centuries, the land that became the nation of Israel in 1948 had been the possession of Muslims, Christian Arabs, and Jews, living together in harmony as part of the Ottoman Empire but considering themselves Palestinian.

In 1936, a rumored plan for a Jewish homeland circulated in the Middle East. This increased local stress and resulted in sporadic guerilla street fighting between Arabs and Jews. As the debate over a Jewish homeland dragged on, frustration over the competing priorities of the

British, Jews, and Arabs resulted in the first outbreak of Middle Eastern terror. The local independence movement led by the Jewish groups *Irgun* and *Lechi* was determined to end the British mandate. The world first heard of Palestinian freedom fighters when Jews attacked the British, not when Arabs started fighting Jews. On July 22, 1946, the Jewish freedom party Irgun blew up the King David Hotel, the seat of British government offices and the quarters for military staff in the center of Jerusalem. The Irgun sent an advance warning to the British authorities but were reportedly snubbed by the rebuke that the British didn't take orders from Jews. Ninety-two people died, and the British Parliament declared the event a murderous outrage.

This troubling story is one of many examples of the historical events that have set the stage for continuing international misunderstanding and tragic loss of life. Given the thousands of lives lost and thousands more in jeopardy, the following facts should be considered with grave and prayerful concern.

The Quest for a Jewish Homeland

From 1940 to 1955, Fraser Wilkins was the foreign service officer of Near East Affairs for the United States Department of State. It was his responsibility to facilitate the communication process within his area of government, as well as with outside groups and international agencies. Since it was Wilkins's role as the State Department Officer to know intimately what was going on in Near East affairs during this critical time period, he was in the key place to have full access to all information regarding the formation of Israel from an American perspective. We are fortunate that a representative of the Harry S. Truman Library and Museum tape-recorded an interview with Fraser Wilkins in 1975.[16] The material in this section is based on Wilkins's first-hand experience.

The creation of a Jewish homeland was a long, drawn-out, and highly complex process. The discussion originated in 1897 with an article by philosopher Theodore Herzl, a German-Jewish intellectual. Herzl feared that the Hebrew faith and tradition would be lost if the Jews continued to be scattered over the world. If not gathered once again in a homeland, they were in grave danger of being assimilated into the cultures where they lived.

In 1917, Chaim Weizmann, a scientist, statesman, and Zionist leader, persuaded the British government to issue a statement favoring the establishment of a Jewish homeland. This statement became known as the Balfour Declaration and was in part approved as an expression of appreciation for Jewish cooperation during World War I. The declaration "approved the concept of a Jewish homeland as long as it did not disturb the Arabs."[17]

In 1922, the League of Nations ratified the Balfour Declaration and gave Britain a mandate to govern Palestine in the absence of Ottoman rule. This news inspired Jewish optimism. Jews immediately began to immigrate into Palestine; the pace accelerated in the mid-1930s, when German Jews began to flee Nazi oppression. A swelling tide of refugees also pushed in from Eastern Europe, where some had learned political activism from the communists. They came to build a new nation by whatever means it took. As the buildup continued, the original Palestinian Jews and Arabs responded with hostility. The British in turn sought to restrict Jewish immigration, as it was threatening the ethnic balance of Palestine and destabilizing the area.

It became increasingly difficult to maintain order. Despite US pressure to continue Jewish refugee immigration, in 1939 the British issued a notice that Jewish immigration was now curtailed. The old Jewish/Arab establishment was pleased, but the promoters of a Jewish homeland felt betrayed and looked to the United States for support. President Franklin D. Roosevelt was sympathetic to the Jewish immigrants' concerns but assured the Arab nations that the United States would not intervene without consulting both sides.

After Harry S. Truman assumed the presidency upon Roosevelt's death, Truman made it clear that he accepted the Balfour Declaration and believed that "in light of the Holocaust, oppressed Jews needed a homeland."[18] At length, an Anglo-American Committee of Inquiry was established by the United Nations. In April of 1946, the committee submitted recommendations that a trustee agreement aimed at bringing Jews and Arabs together be established by the UN, that full Jewish immigration be allowed into Palestine, and that two autonomous states be established with a strong central government to control Jerusalem, Bethlehem, and the Negev, the southernmost section of Palestine. The recommendations potentially resolved many issues, but resulted in one unanimous response: no one was pleased. The recommendations gave everybody something, but gave nobody all they wanted. All parties resoundingly rejected the UN committee report, a foreshadowing of the controversy surrounding many such attempts over the next sixty years.

As the UN appeared to be doing little to implement their unpopular decision or explore other options, the international community refrained from direct intervention. Meanwhile, the restless Zionist Jews, angered by the British refusal of more refugee resettlement, took matters into their own hands. They began serious civil protests and furtive attempts to disrupt the flow of the local British government. As mentioned earlier, it was at this point, on July 22, 1946, that the radical Jewish freedom party, the Irgun, planted explosives in the King David Hotel. They gave the British a warning to vacate, which was sarcastically ignored. The explosives were detonated, with a reported death toll of ninety-two, including British officers, Arabs, and several Jews.[19]

Arab/Jewish communications collapsed, and the British, furious over the terrorist activity of the Jewish freedom fighters and weary of the thankless task of trying to maintain order within the restive Palestinian population, indicated to the UN that they were going to terminate their mandate early. On April 2, 1947, Britain requested that the UN establish the Special Committee on Palestine—UNSCOP. After four months of negotiation, the Special Committee recommended what became known as Resolution 181: The British mandate was to end, and Palestine was to be partitioned into two states.

Painful as it is to acknowledge, the urgent concern to create a Jewish homeland was not primarily altruistic. I was a teenage infantryman in Europe when Hitler's death camps were liberated. The horror was unbelievable. We who were in the area sensed that the responsibility lay not only with Hitler and his German followers, but in some ways with the free world as well. For years, nations of the West had been aware that Jewish lives were in grave jeopardy. The United States made little, if any, serious effort to intervene.

For instance, on June 4, 1939, the US Coast Guard turned back from a port on the coast of Florida the SS *St. Louis* with 907 German-Jewish refugees aboard. After safe entries to ports in Cuba and Canada were denied, the ship returned to Europe with its desperate human cargo. Later research showed that 260 of those people died in Nazi death camps.[20] Residual guilt for such tragic disregard for human life played a key role in what was to come.

Jewish refugees became an acknowledged concern of the United States only after the bombing of Pearl Harbor in December 1941. By 1948, when the horror of Hitler's death camps was in full display, the Jewish Homeland Resolution 181 was under debate. By then, more thousands of Jewish refugees were crowding into central Europe in flight from Stalin. Food was in short supply, but there was more than enough guilt to go around. The UN was plagued with a major dilemma: how to resolve what was quietly termed "the Jewish problem" of postwar Europe.

As is often the case amid a social crisis, the pressure to resolve one critical issue often creates another. The UN-proposed Jewish Homeland Plan had one glaring weakness. In the process of responding to the pain and guilt of the Holocaust, a new cause for guilt was blindly ignored. In their planning and negotiation, although they broadly consulted even the Arab nations, the committee failed to carefully listen to and consult with the Palestinian Arabs. The proposed plan benefited Europe by solving a critical refugee problem. It benefited the Jews by providing them a homeland. But the proposed plan severely jeopardized the Palestinian Arabs. Some six hundred thousand Muslim and Christian Arabs were being expected to vacate a significant portion of their homeland and crowd in with their neighbors on the portion of Palestine that would be left for them. The plan did not include satisfactory compensation for loss of property or the building of attractive, new communities. No equitable relocation plan was seriously proposed, let alone carefully negotiated.

The response of the Council of the Arab League to the UNSCOP proposal to partition Palestine into two states was unequivocal rejection. The Council sent a directive to their member nations to immediately move troops to the Palestinian border. In the United States, this period was early in the cold war with the USSR. The American Joint Chiefs of Staff warned that a forced partition of Palestine could encourage Russian sympathy with the Arab states and place at risk a continued oil supply. General George Marshall, the Secretary of State, advised against a forced division of Palestine, as well as any unilateral recognition of

Israel as an independent nation, believing the Middle Eastern situation was too volatile.

In the meantime, President Truman was under great pressure from the members of his own party and from the Zionist-American community. He admitted that he had received some thirty thousand pieces of mail urging the establishment of a Jewish homeland. He said that he had refused to read it, as he believed that the UN committee's work should proceed without interference. He also refused the request to meet with Chaim Weizmann, the president of the Zionist movement. Having been directly rebuffed, Weizmann made another effort to see the president. The president's longtime Jewish friend from his World War I military unit and later his business partner, Eddie Jacobson, came unannounced to see Truman. As a friend, he pleaded with the president simply to talk with Weizmann. This approach succeeded. Jacobson introduced the two men, and Weizmann made his point: "The tragedy of the Holocaust must be addressed. The solution to the pain and grief of the Jews [is] the creation of a Jewish homeland."[21]

As the president said after his visit with Weizmann, "In light of the Holocaust, the Jews deserved a homeland." It was a solution that seemed fair. It would cost us little or nothing, or so it was thought.[22] What seems to have been overlooked by nearly everyone is what it would cost the Arab citizens of Palestine.

After a conversation with Clark Clifford, his personal counsel, and General George Marshall, Secretary of State, President Truman directed the State Department to support the UN plan to divide Palestine. General Marshall reluctantly obeyed the president's order and gave the message to his state department staff to support UN Resolution 181 when it came before the UN for debate.

On November 29, 1947, after significant debate, the UN General Assembly passed Resolution 181, approving the division of Palestine into three entities: a Jewish state, an Arab state, and an International Zone around Jerusalem. Again the plan met with hostility, especially on the part of the Arab nations. In the following five months, there was grave uncertainty as to how to proceed. Britain felt abandoned. The British responsibility to maintain order within Palestine was growing more dangerous and complex. The UN offered the British no direct help or resolution. The Jewish freedom fighters, having already blown up the

King David Hotel, were a constant threat within Jerusalem, and the Arab armies around the perimeter were unnerving.

With no specific plan to implement Resolution 181 coming from the UN, the British found their position untenable. Without waiting for the official end of their mandate of responsibility, on the morning of May 14, 1948, the British pulled all their forces out of Israel. At midnight on May 14, with no authorization from the UN, the Jewish Provisional Government proclaimed the new state of Israel. Since their action was unauthorized, in itself it had no binding authority.

Midnight in Israel is 6 p.m. in Washington, DC, and at 6:11 p.m., President Harry Truman made one of the key political moves of the twentieth century. With no formal consultation with Congress or official notification to the State Department or the US delegation at the UN, President Truman provided an unauthorized but nonetheless symbolic stamp of approval. He formally signed a statement recognizing Israel as a sovereign nation. Much to the anger of the State Department and the UN delegation, the president released his statement to the press prior to informing them. The resulting crisis was a foregone conclusion.

In the Middle East, the response was immediate. The Arab states attacked Israel and were met with startling force. When diplomats achieved a truce, Israel's forces had advanced to a position giving them thirty percent more land than had been assigned to them in the original UN proposal. The Arab people in many cases fled before the Jewish advance. In other cases they were forced off their land and put into relocation centers hastily erected by the United Nations. Resolution 181 had not only created a homeland for the Jewish people, but it had also torn away a homeland from a half million Muslim and Christian Arab people.

To recap: United Nations Resolution 181 was implemented in part by extralegal activity. The first of the three provisions of 181—providing a Jewish homeland—was implemented by bypassing a specific UN official blessing and unilaterally announcing Israel's own independence via an immediate US confirmation by President Truman. Beyond this, the UN allowed the other two provisions of Resolution 181—an independent Arab state and a UN zone internationalizing Jerusalem and its vicinity—to be forfeited. This occurred because:

1. The British left their trust mandate, originally established to govern and protect the people of Palestine, earlier than agreed on. Thus they left the door open for the Jewish Provisional Authority to divide the territory and deny the original residents full legal access to their property.

2. The Jewish Provisional Authority of Palestine, a quasi-governmental entity, unilaterally declared Israel to be a sovereign state. At the time, this was an act without legal provision or binding authority, since the UN had not as yet officially implemented Resolution 181.

3. The president of the United States, against the counsel of his own appointed advisors for international and military affairs, abused his powers exercised under the informal advice and consent process that exists between the legislative and administrative branches of our democratic government. He also circumvented proper UN process and acknowledged Israel as a sovereign state without consultation with the UN.

This is the background of the Israel/Palestinian stalemate that has continued to cause tragic loss of life on both sides and international tension and consternation for over sixty years. It remains today a primary provocation that fuels the fire of terrorist hostility. Certainly, irresponsible terrorist acts have been wrongfully committed in response to this hostility. But the larger issue is that for all this time, the international community has failed to respond forcefully to this basic injustice.

Two things appear clear: Jewish people needed and deserved a homeland, and Arab people deserved the international respect that would have guaranteed them justice. Neither group was required to respond to the international oversight that the United Nations should have exerted immediately after the illegal declaration of Israel as a sovereign state. How could the United States allow the improper action of our president to stand without making full restitution to the half million Arabs who lost their homeland and their property?

The formation of Israel and the injustices suffered by Palestine and its Arab people are the offenses mentioned most frequently by Osama bin Laden and other apologists for terrorist conduct. Behind these objective issues related to the Palestinian/Israeli crisis are the much more devastating, subjective issues in the human equation of pain and destitution over the past sixty years.

The emotionally destructive power of this continuing conflict becomes clear to anyone willing to look with empathy at the situation through the eyes of a grieving Jewish or Arab father who has watched his children deprived of a challenging education and a peaceful home, and then go, as he once went, to fight in an endless battle, possibly to their deaths. It is also clear to anyone willing to look with compassion through the eyes of a mother who has just lifted the body of her bloodied child to her breast as in a traumatized daze she watches the smoke rise from yet another in a series of endless missile raids.

Having studied this period of history, lived through the times it covers, visited Israel, and talked to knowledgeable people, I am deeply convinced that what occurred in the formation of the state of Israel was a noble cause pursued with undue haste by tragically inept diplomacy and misguided administrative leadership. The ineptitude of US foreign policy in 1948 and over the ensuing years has allowed a recurring cycle of death and suffering. This is the tragic prelude to the criminal travesty of the 9/11 attacks, as acknowledged by their perpetrator, Osama bin Laden. A verse from scripture seems ironically appropriate: "As I have seen, those who plow iniquity and sow trouble reap the same" (Job 4:8).

The Aftermath of UN Resolution 181

As the dust settled in Palestine after May 14, 1948, the UN placed thousands of Christian and Muslim Arabs fleeing from their homes in what were intended to be temporary relocation centers. Without any definite plan for implementation, the West assumed that the displaced people would be assimilated back into other Middle Eastern countries. This, of course, has rarely occurred, and for two basic reasons: The people themselves resisted the idea of relocation, and other countries were not eager to assimilate such large numbers of people. They were uprooted from homes that they, their parents, and their grandparents had built and loved. Why would they want to leave, and who would take them if they did? These refugee relocation compounds continue to exist today at an annual cost of millions of dollars to the UN, much of which is paid by the American taxpayer.

With no self-determination and no sense of hope or justice, over the years these refugees became both victims of and participants in organized hate. The Wahhabi hate mongers used them in raids and suicide attacks to further destabilize the Middle East. Saudi Arabian literature and evangelistic promoters of violence were sent to encourage groups like Hamas to fan the flames of vengeance. For the terrorists, there appeared but one course of justice, one resolution: the end of Israel.

During years of attempted Israeli and Palestinian peace proposals, the original injustice has never been adequately addressed. The option of another Palestinian state, far smaller and with no reimbursement for past crimes, is not justice. Millions of dollars of aid have been poured into Israel, and a creative, prosperous nation has emerged. Millions have also been poured into Palestinian relocation camps and three generations of detainees have been fed, poorly housed, and minimally educated. The aftermath of Resolution 181 for Palestinian Christians and Muslims was not only the sense of a lost state. The Palestinians lost their homes, their livelihoods, their history, and, yes, their integrity. Their stubborn resistance to a settlement may appear on the surface to be self-defeating and foolish. Yet, given the facts, it may be a last, desperate attempt to restore a sense of shattered identity.

There is another more disturbing aspect to the issue of Palestinian peace. The power brokers behind Hamas and the originators of the PLO simply may not want a settlement. Hamas, with Sunni origins in Saudi Arabia, has for years harassed Israel with a continuing barrage of suicide bombings and other forms of aggression. Now, with some embarrassment to those of us who trust the democratic process, Hamas has gained a begrudged acceptance through the political process. The perceived injustice of Resolution 181 continues to give Hamas's leaders a rationale to build their support base and perpetrate hate crimes around the world. If the Palestinians had been given true restitution and a generous opportunity to rebuild and flourish, the Wahhabis would have lost the trump card in their playing hand of reasons to promote hatred against the United States.

The tragedy in establishing the state of Israel was not the concept but the blind haste and amazing ineptitude of its implementation. After the clear assurance in the original Balfour Declaration that the rights of the Arabs would be safeguarded, scant attention was given to the moral implications of Resolution 181. The Jewish people deserved a new start, but neither they nor the Arabs deserved the endlessly unresolved physical and moral crisis thrust upon them. Although they both initially generated much of the chaos, the basic problems in the Middle East that continue to be deadly now cannot be charged to either Jews or Arabs. The issue more correctly rests with the moral callousness of world leadership, which in apathy has allowed the situation to fester with no resolution in sight.

While neither Jews nor Arabs are free of blame for the sixty years of chaos, it is the international community, represented by their United Nations memberships, who are charged with approving and implementing Resolution 181. Further, it is the United States, starting with the presumption of President Truman, which has failed to maintain a balanced support of both Jews and Arabs during the long years of tension. A full appraisal of the moral issues involved must be the beginning point of any new effort to secure Middle Eastern peace. All the while, the radical terrorist movement has used the plight of the Arabs as their cause célèbre for promoting anti-Western and anti-Israeli hate and destruction. In other words, the radicals have appropriated the anguish of Palestine to promote their own objectives. The perception that the United States favors Israel plays into their diabolical purpose.

The pain of Palestine is a major part of the international dilemma of the twenty-first century. We live in an increasingly shrinking neighborhood—that of Planet Earth. What affects one affects all. How interesting that long ago the prophetic voice of God described the issue well, "For they sow the wind, and they shall reap the whirlwind" (Hosea 8:7). The Wahhabi corruption of a religious faith has now come to be a death curse that endangers our world. As bin Laden reminded us after his deadly triumph of 9/11, "Neither America nor anyone who lives there will enjoy safety until safety becomes a reality for us living in Palestine."[23]

Section IV–
A Faith Response to the Challenge of Terrorism

> You have heard that it was said, "You shall love your neighbor and hate your enemy." But I say to you, Love your enemies and pray for those who persecute you, so that you may be children of your Father in heaven; for He makes His sun rise on the evil and on the good, and sends rain on the righteous and on the unrighteous. Be perfect, therefore, as your heavenly Father is perfect. (Matthew 5:43–45, 48)

The provocative words of Vatican II, issued sincerely by the Roman Catholic Church in the mid-twentieth century, serve as a point of entry into the challenge of Jesus to love our enemies: "Since in the course of centuries not a few quarrels and hostilities have arisen between Christians and Moslems, this sacred synod urges all to forget the past and to work sincerely for mutual understanding."[1]

This declaration gives voice to our own concern for social justice, moral welfare, peace, and freedom. Two major flaws limit its effectiveness. First, this plea urges progress starting with the appeal that all parties forget the past. Second, it encourages moral engagement as an ideological commitment, without offering specific, tangible steps for local community involvement.

Is there reason for greater hope today? Can we begin the process of reconciliation by ignoring the causes and the pain of past disunity? Can progress emerge from dialogue that ends with ideological commitment but spells out no tangible steps for corrective action?

The novelist Joyce Carol Oates responds hopefully, or perhaps wistfully, to the despair and pain of 9/11 in her mid-December 2001 editorial: "Amnesia seeps into the crevices of our brains and amnesia heals.... The future is ever young, ever forgetting the gravest truths of the past."[2]

We are an optimistic people. We move into the future, claiming a better tomorrow. Yet the questions remain: Should we forget? Should we as a people forget the nineteenth-century March of Tears, where seven thousand Cherokee Indians died during a forced cross-country trek as the federal government attempted to resettle an entire Native American nation in the plains of Oklahoma? We should not forget such injustice; we should not forget the brutality perpetrated against the natives of this great land.

Should we forget the great tragedy of World War I, where nine million soldiers and eleven million civilians died in the cataclysm of Europe that settled nothing? When we tried to ignore those bloody battles, the result was the Treaty at Versailles, which laid the foundation for World War II, established a pattern for Middle Eastern colonialism, and set the stage for terrorist hostility and violence.

In an effort to block this natural forgetting process, the 9/11 Memorial Team has worked for years amid deep anguish and frequent controversy to plan and build a memorial at Ground Zero intended to keep the memory fresh. The hope is that deep spiritual love, repentance, and restoration can change the geo-political landscape in ways that will neutralize the hate and build a new ideological base for a future of justice and peace. The more recent controversy over building a Muslim community center and mosque nearby presented an opportunity for Christians, Jews, and Muslims to explore their prejudices and displace fear with love, a task much more complicated and important than mere tolerance.

Ideally, we should recognize in the face of the average, faithful Muslim a potential ally in our struggle for world peace. Why? "Because the power of ideas that can call men and women to make great sacrifices can only be trumped by the power of more compelling ideas that summon forth nobler sacrifices."[3] Ideas are what drive terrorist action. Only strong, spirit-directed ideas have the strength to replace flawed concepts. It will take nobler ideas to dislodge the terrorists and move us toward peace. True Islam offers us a bridge for authentic outreach to our enemy. It has greater access to the hearts and minds of vulnerable youths in distant Islamic countries. Then a bond of trust and friendship among Christians, Jews, and Muslims will be our best resource for bridging the gap between the uncommitted of our world and a hope for peace.

We must share the truth God has entrusted to us with all people and trust God to affirm our effort through the power of his love. Just as a faithful Jew is our ally in battle, so too is a faithful Muslim. The Prophet Muhammad taught that his vision was not a new religion but a continuation of the revelations found in the Old Testament and the Gospels. His vision was that God wants all human life to be called together in united submission to God. Jesus declared the same goal in his closing statement on the Mount of Ascension (Matthew 28:19–20). In our concluding chapters, we will explore the possibility that each of these future visions referred to in theology as the eschatological plan of God offers a common truth that we can all embrace.

In this book, we have considered a combination of historic and religious facts that Muslims in particular, but also Christians and Jews, might find stressful and provocative. The intent has been to recall the past to open the way to healthy dialogue and courageous change in the future. Open to self-criticism, informed by the wisdom of others, and inspired by the common foundations of our faith traditions, let us take bold new steps toward justice and peace. Recommitted to the love of God and neighbor, we can boldly recast our political policy, opening doors of understanding and trust.

Chapter 11

Personal Spiritual Preparation

The burden of world terror seems stunning. We can easily slip into denial: close the book, change the subject, turn up the TV, and escape. What can one person do? We don't have to look far; the love of God and neighbor begins within. Live a spiritually aware life. Reach out to others. Support family. Reclaim the high moral ground. If you believe that God is calling you to a life of love, these are the places to start. Are you willing to accept the challenge? If so, you could change the world.

The present world crisis of radical religious hate confronts our time just as the cold war did in the 1950s through the 1970s. The cold war crisis was easier to deal with because its focus was so much clearer. The ideology of godless communism had an obvious face and a geographical location to go with it.

It is crucial that we recognize the radical terror movement of today did not originate in response to the offenses of the West. Rather, Islamic reformers began their efforts in Egypt and Saudi Arabia, where they attempted to purify and restore a Muslim faith-based system to those secular governments. Only later did this reformation process take on an anti-Western life of its own. With those issues sharply in focus, our response can be more authentic, hopeful, and helpful.

Living a Spiritually Aware Life

Being able to distinguish between faithful Muslims and members of the Wahhabi radical cult is key to managing our fear. This awareness will also safeguard us from slipping into a sloppy response that labels the Islamic faith in general as the enemy. Such generalized condemnation not only distorts our focus and diminishes our effectiveness, but also undermines our democratic principles. To say that as a nation we uphold religious freedom only to deny it to a particular group makes us fair game for charges of hypocrisy and plays into the hands of the radicals.

To blame modern Islam in general for problems originating in tragic mistakes of the past is to miss the point and deny the possibility of an honest resolution. If we are to fight the war on terror, we need to understand the real issues. In *The Fog of War*, referring to the tragedy of the Vietnam War, former Secretary of Defense Robert McNamara states, "Success in any war requires that we understand our enemy and their goals."[1]

The suffering in the unresolved Middle Eastern situation should reinforce our determination to live fully aware lives, spiritually attuned to opportunities to be creatively useful. Resolution 181 should serve as a vivid reminder in both local and international policy development to consistently check facts and guard against easy solutions that may have hidden consequences. The commendable vision but short-circuited process that led to the formation of Israel reveals how well-intentioned, misguided solutions to complex problems can be co-opted by radicals. They, in turn, twist the issues and destroy innocent people as they promote their cause of confusion and social destabilization.

The ideological issues now are even subtler because of the general public confusion about Islam. The cold war is our closest historical illustration. In the 1980s, it was important to understand the ideology and goals of the USSR. But the public also needed to understand the super-heated, anticommunist patriotism of the McCarthy era and the irrational hate campaign that it generated. Misdirecting the focus of our concern, now as then, could prove self-destructive.

Grasping competing ideological issues is vitally important. The future of international peace lies in the balance. As people of faith, we need to be deeply devoted to the truth of our faith and practice it with joyful diligence. Likewise, we need to understand the central spiritual foundation of Islam so that we can distinguish it from the destructive, counterfeit message of the radicals.

Openness to Islam does not mean that Christians or Jews need to compromise a total commitment to their faith. But all of us can joyfully affirm that the message of the Prophet Muhammad, when truly presented, has creatively dislodged the forces of superstition and hatred and brought many human beings a productive peace and monotheistic morality.

Christians need not hesitate to share their faith with either Jew or Muslim as long as we are faithful to the spirit of Christ and open to offering a similar courtesy to the person with whom we share. God is quite capable of defending the truth as long as we are capable of living it. If we are open, our Lord can use us to build new alliances and extend the circle of his gracious influence. In this spirit, Islam is a potential partner in the peace process.

One-to-One Relationships

During the past two years, Muslim families from Turkey, Egypt, Indonesia, and Bosnia have welcomed me into their homes. We met after I contacted the local Islamic Dialogue Center. My prayerful purpose was to be a loving friend and quiet witness to the grace of God. The witness I received in return reflected the monotheistic traditions of Abraham, Moses, and Jesus as interpreted by the Prophet Muhammad. God was present in these natural experiences of new friendship. Such interfaith contacts can open the way for God to change the hearts and awareness of a confused and violent world, building new communities of understanding—one family at a time.

The world is clustered at our doorstep. All it takes to answer God's call to love our neighbor is stepping across the threshold. It won't always be easy. Sometimes it will involve sacrifice. But by taking the initiative, we discover the joy of deep, spiritual service. Moving beyond our uncertainty brings us into the sustaining love of God's grace. It is in creative action that the fear and uncertainty leave us and the joy begins.

The Gospel invites us to love and offer devotion to the Spirit of God. Only then can we live out God's call to love even our enemies. Key passages from the Bible guide our focus:

> Beloved, let us love one another, because love is
> from God; everyone who loves is born of God
> and knows God. Whoever does not love does
> not know God, for God is love. (1 John 4:7–8)

> If any want to become my followers, let them
> deny themselves and take up their cross daily
> and follow me. (Luke 9:23)

> Therefore I tell you, do not worry about your
> life, what you will eat ... or about your body,
> what you will wear ... But strive first for the
> kingdom of God and his righteousness, and
> all these things will be given to you as well.
> (Matthew 6:25, 33)

Maintaining a personal relationship with God is the very essence of human existence. It is why we were created. As the old Westminster Catechism challenges us, "The chief end of man, [the true purpose of life] is to worship God and to enjoy Him forever." Whatever price in energy, stress, time, or inconvenience may be involved, our openness to the living presence of God in our lives is a benefit in time and in eternity worthy of whatever it may seem to cost.

The mystery of the Gospel seems at first a divestiture—laying aside one's self-focus and ego. Unencumbered by self, we are free to adopt a new identity, new relationships, and a new vocation. The gifts of the spirit and the transformative presence of the living Christ refashion our lives. To resist this transforming love is to lose sight of our ultimate human potential.

Author Ron Hansen, interviewed by Amy Frykholm for *Christian Century,* makes the point that faith involves times of doubt and uncertainty. Hansen declares:

> I have a priest friend who points out that the
> opposite of faith is not doubt but certainty. I
> think God intended that—it is a way of making
> us creative instead of smug in our belief. God
> plants in us the seed to love and worship God,
> and the seed is enough to make us want to seek

God out, but not enough to fully get there. That
reaching, that striving, is what God is really
interested in—that creative activity that all of
us should pursue.[2]

Because we dare to live this mystical faith in uncertainty, we humbly
move toward spiritual maturity ourselves, while patiently loving others
as Christ has loved us.

Expressing the Love of God in Our Inner Circle

From examining our personal relationship with God, we move now to
the next level in our spiritual preparation. It is important to recognize
that nothing we do in the world is fully authentic unless it reflects what
we do in our relationships with those loved ones whom we see, listen
to, and touch day by day. We model our convictions and express our
purpose in the family circle.

A design for faithful living begins at home. It is here that we establish
a pattern of life that reflects the purpose, peace, and spiritual power God
desires for our total life. Just think how you and your family would
benefit if together you agreed to follow these practices at home:

- We pledge to affirm our spiritual call and review the details
  of our mission.
- We pledge to practice the spirit of our call in our daily
  interactions.
- We pledge to model attitudes and words of love in our daily
  contacts.
- We pledge to express differences in the spirit of love.
- We pledge to listen to and affirm each other with empathy
  and sensitivity.
- We pledge to share the routine duties necessary for an
  ordered, healthy life of peace.
- We pledge to plan opportunities for group fun, relaxation,
  and entertainment.
- We pledge to provide regular opportunities to explore moral
  and spiritual values.
- We pledge to share gracious hospitality where those dear to
  us or in need find warmth and love.

- We pledge to plan a family pattern of generous financial stewardship.
- We pledge to practice the habit of praying for and with our family daily and worshiping together weekly.
- We pledge to evaluate the style and relationships of family life at regular intervals.

Many of these practices may already be taken for granted among serious Christians. In any case, designing a supportive family system of spiritual development is an important aid in encouraging the disciplines of the Christian life. We love the Lord with inner devotion, but we learn to serve the Lord through outer discipline and communal support. Of special note is the bonding of nurture and mission. Perhaps the discipline of the home is the best environment to clarify and apply this basic truth. Two concepts, but our Lord engaged them simultaneously.

Reclaiming the High Moral Ground

Christians need to address the serious decline of morality in society, both at home and in the church. Parents need to model consistent standards of morality to avoid sending mixed messages to their children. When outside responsibilities seem overwhelming, parents should seek support from their church. Spiritually mature mentors can make a big difference in these cases.

Congregations need to evaluate their institution's formal faith formation process for children and youth. In many congregations, joining the church or participating in the confirmation class is viewed as a rite of passage. Many of these Sunday school graduates have never seen a deeply committed home or a congregation involved in spiritual nurture or hands-on mission. At this impressionable stage of life, is it any wonder they find their church boring and irrelevant? They have never felt the excitement or been part of the adventure of their church creatively living as the body of Christ (Ephesians 4:12).

We must slay the twin demons of moral apathy and spiritual complacency. The alternative is to settle for a religious style of passive tolerance that witnesses to cozy conformity, does little in spiritual formation, and accomplishes less in hands-on mission work. This approach to "church" is a denial of the Gospel that regularly plays out in our national life. In contrast, motivated, spirit-led leadership in politics, the professions, banking, industry, education, and commerce is the urgent need of our time.

The Church needs to reclaim the high moral ground for young people, guiding them to claim lives of moral purity and spiritually relevant choices. Our young people urgently need to sense their role within the church as a vital part of the body of Christ (Ephesians 1:22 and 4:11–16). The teen years can be a time filled with challenging instruction and exciting spiritual adventure. When we make Christian education a priority, impressionable teens will come to see their Church as the place to be.

One Among Many

The wonder of the civil rights movement of the 1950s and 1960s gives us pause to consider the potential of spirit-directed individual power. Civil change had been brewing for a long time, but the movement went national when one woman acted at the spirit-directed moment. Rosa Parks sat secure in her seat on that bus, calmly defying law and culture, before she was finally carried away to jail. In turn came the response of a young preacher, Martin Luther King, Jr., who led widely attended prayer meetings, a costly bus boycott, and marches disruptive to the status quo, until he was also carried away to jail. Finally, President Lyndon Johnson encouraged and signed civil rights legislation that a conscience-stricken Congress was morally compelled to pass. The courage of one woman served as a vital spark that fired the flame of radical change.

If a spiritually alive democracy thrives on the vision of its leadership, and it does, the question becomes: Where do we find such leaders? They are sitting at our dinner tables and in the pews of our churches. Authentic Christian homes and vibrant congregations are the two sources, working together, from which leaders will step forth. They are the children and grandchildren that we inspire today. These new leaders will be raised up from among us, equipped and deployed to strengthen our nation.

Consider the thoughts of author Lee C. Camp as he refers to such ordinary Christian people obedient to God's purpose:

Jesus called his disciples to participate in a kingdom that was invading human history, a kingdom so present you could reach out and touch it, a new order in their very midst. "For, in fact, the kingdom of God is among you" (Luke 17:21).… The way of the kingdom was not the way of power and might, but the way of suffering servanthood, a real alternative to the ways of the rebellious principalities and powers that naively, if not arrogantly, think they are in control of human history.… Because of the powers undone by Christ's death and Christ's way vindicated by the resurrection, we are invited to participate in the kingdom that celebrates that victory and lives out its immediate implications: as he loved, so we love.[3]

Strong Christian families bonded together in vital local congregations create:

- Challenging centers of faith formation
- Cultural confrontation, countering greed and immorality
- Social transformation, modeling justice and peace

Sustained by God's love, such churches will be change agents that:

- Welcome strangers
- Encourage the marginalized
- Serve the needy

The compassionate Gospel of such churches will:

- Share the good news of healing love and saving grace
- Bless every community where they are found
- Witness abroad to the families and friends of local people who are blessed

This is the way to peace. It is to this high calling that we respond. As the Apostle Paul vividly declared: "Christ in you, the hope of glory!"

Chapter 12

Radical Love in Community

The first response to the call of God is inward, a personal stirring of love, purity, and joy. The second response is naturally expressed in the intimacy of the family circle, where it is explored, modeled, and then applied in the life of a congregation. Now we are ready to explore the third response, deployment, where the congregation moves out into service, bridging social barriers and building healthy and peaceful communities.

Jesus spent little of his time with the disciples in passive training. They were soon out in the field of ministry: listening, watching, and participating. After the resurrection, Jesus returned to the disciples. He overshadowed them with the power of the Spirit, which they did not understand or appreciate until they were obediently engaged in active ministry. Finally, he commissioned them to make disciples in concentric circles from the immediate environment of Jerusalem, on out progressively to the ends of the earth.

Our Lord's command to "love one another as I have loved you" calls us to radical commitment. Our relationship with others is a gospel call to replicate the relationship Jesus had with the disciples. Billy Sunday, the fiery, early-nineteenth-century evangelist, is widely claimed to have said, "Our spiritual problem is not that Christian faith has failed, but that it has not been fully tried." That is the challenge before us today.

The Critical Nature of Our Emerging Challenge

Our communities must courageously acknowledge a clear distinction between the misguided terrorists influenced by Wahhabi radicals and the faithful American Muslim citizens who are our neighbors. Only people with a strong faith commitment will be equal to the complexity of this task. The difficulty is not so much the impending danger from without as it is the cultural challenge of confronting the moral drift of our society and the anti-Muslim prejudice promoted by our misunderstanding and media-inspired fear.

First, we face an urgent need to stabilize our moral erosion and restore integrity at the center of American society. This is a major spiritual challenge for us as parents, grandparents, and teachers, and is a challenge as well for our centers of spiritual formation. Moral laxity poses a major threat to the social well-being of our society, to say nothing of the offense to our calling as people of faith, committed to sexual decency and purity. It is a sad state when a person like Osama bin Laden berates us for moral indecency, as he did in this speech "to the Americans" in 2003:

> You are a nation that exploits women like consumer products or advertising tools, calling upon customers to purchase them. You use women to serve passengers, visitors, and strangers to increase your profit margins. You then rant that you support the liberation of women. You are a nation that practices the trade of sex in all its forms directly and indirectly. Giant corporations and establishments are established on this, under the name of art, entertainment, tourism, and freedom, and other deceptive names that you attribute to it.[1]

Who is God calling to be involved in this enterprise of restoring spiritual health and building peaceful communities across faith and ethnic boundaries? The answer is simple but startling. We are all called to play a part in defeating the evil of international terrorism. How are we to do this? The call of Christ has always been to provide havens of welcome to the stranger and the needy. The only difference now

163

is that the call appears more urgent as it mingles with our stress and uncertainty.

Terror is the active side of destruction, and apathy is the passive side. Both participate in the negative process. Every person committed to peace, every household committed to God's purpose, and every congregation committed to the Kingdom of God is needed to engage in this united effort to build a new world of peace and understanding. *So we are speaking of total deployment.*

The terrorism challenge, although a fearsome dilemma, also has the potential to create a tremendous blessing. As we joyfully declare the love and peace of Jesus and live sacrificial lives of compassion among our neighbors, these six to seven million Muslims and millions more of other immigrant people who receive our love are all potential witnesses.

Across the Middle East, through Europe, Central and South America, Indonesia, India, the Philippines, and Africa, this worldwide flow of influence is presently in our midst. As the transforming love of Christ is lived joyfully and shared compassionately, we will have an impact on the faith awareness of a major segment of the earth. The Gospel will be experienced for what it is: not a Western religion waging wars of retaliation, but the personal message of God's accepting grace, transforming lives, and rebuilding communities.

Christian-Muslim Interaction and the Terrorist Threat

Those with contacts in Europe often warn Americans that the social unrest and occasional violence related to Muslim communities there will soon occur in the United States. But this overlooks a basic difference in the two immigrant populations. The majority of the large immigrant Muslim populations in Europe are working people who have migrated mostly from Turkey and Morocco in response to the need for unskilled labor. They have usually been housed in segregated areas, with little attention given to assimilation or appreciation of the local culture.

Although many Muslim immigrants have now lived in Europe for two or more generations, they are not an integral part of the culture. Their young people suffer from the sense of being strangers in the land of their birth. With little sense of identity with the mores of the country, the young people from these ghetto communities are easy targets of radical leaders. Internal unrest, especially in large cities of France and the outskirts of London, has been a natural result.

In contrast to the European situation, Muslims entering the United States are usually from the professional, technical, and managerial classes of Muslim society. They immigrated with independent funds and chose to live among the population in general. Their children attend local schools and participate in community youth events. Until 9/11, the integration of Muslims in the United States was fairly uneventful.

As was true with earlier European immigrants, the social centers of the new Muslim population are places of worship. Many are active in the little-understood Islamic Friday prayer services at community mosques. The children attend Saturday or Sunday spiritual training programs, just as Jewish and Christian children attend their places of worship.

Immediately after 9/11, however, fear spread among the some six million Muslims who live in the United States. Although the Muslim community made wide disclaimers totally disavowing the radical philosophy of the terrorists, this fact was not widely publicized. The unlikely possibility of an al Qaeda operative in our midst furthered the perceived threat and affected our perceptions of the general Islamic population.

As we seek to engage in local outreach, these issues should be familiar to us. Our role can only be a matter of supportive response to their distress, just as many of them have responded to our pain regarding the tragedy of 9/11. A new Muslim friend may insist that the actions of the terrorists on 9/11 were not representative of true Islam. More often, he or she will assume that we realize that to be true. We are then in a position to listen to their story and learn about Islam without defensiveness. This may open the way for us to share our own faith story. The key to the success of this model of friendly exchange is a version of the Golden Rule—share with others as you would want them to share with you. Carefully listen, gently respond, and let the Spirit of God guide the relationship into deep and committed friendship. In general, Muslims are as misinformed about Christianity as we are about Islam.

It is important that our community-building efforts are not attempts to be "faith neutral." It is only as all parties are free to openly acknowledge their own spiritual commitments that genuine relationships can be developed with deep trust and understanding. These friendships frequently open faith-sharing conversations, and the spirit of God is freed to open doors of understanding and an awareness of our common life goals.

This is not a veiled affirmation of the postmodern supposition that somehow all religions are of equal value. Rather this is an affirmation of the glory of God's revelation in Jesus Christ that should never be compromised. Nor should the person of the Prophet Muhammad be compromised. We should be confident that God is free to use our witness in God's own way, whereas any sense of religious pressure is an offense to the love and freedom found in Jesus.

Modern Islam's Unity and Peace Initiatives

At the time Professor El Fadl published *The Great Theft* in 2005, significant transforming activity appeared to be quietly stabilizing the Muslim world. The inspiration came from the royal court of King Abdullah of Jordan, and the eight Islamic Schools of Jurisprudence developed it. This diverse group of Muslim scholars created a unifying document that clarifies what defines a Muslim.

For the first time in centuries, such a document—The Amman Message—was published in 2006.[2] It contains an interpretive statement defining three foundational Islamic realities of authority, and it is signed by over three hundred leaders of the Muslim world. The signatures represent various Islamic bodies, including the two major sections, Sunni and Shiite, in addition to Salafi reformers, Sufi mystics, and others of the scattered Islamic community.

The document candidly acknowledges the attacks upon the faith from outside forces as well as the distractive action of some who falsely claim identity with the Islamic faith. This new declaration provides an encouraging reason to anticipate a renewed effort within Islam to affirm the mercy, compassion, and peaceful heart of the Prophet's original monotheistic vision. The Amman Message website contains a clear repudiation of the 9/11 attacks and other radical, destructive actions that offend the name of Islam.

Another encouraging development is the letter from the 138 Muslim scholars known as "A Common Word Between Us and You." Addressed to the Pope, to worldwide church leaders by name, and to the Christian community as a whole, this document was released in the fall of 2007.[3] It affirms the basic spiritual commonality found in the Jewish, Christian, and Muslim commitment of love for God and love for neighbor and invites the Christian community to a joint participation in dialogue. It also expresses a deep concern for world peace. The Amman Message and "A Common Word" encourage the possibility of interfaith unity and peaceful cooperation in the future.

For us to totally participate as Christian individuals in such a joint peace effort, we need a humble recognition that Jesus calls us to forgiveness and to an expression of love for neighbor and for enemy (Matthew 5:43–46). This acknowledgment was made clear in a letter of response from leaders of the Christian community in late 2007.[4] Such full Gospel response to God's love requires dependence on his spirit to transform hearts and minds within our Christian community as well as in the Muslim community. Fuller understanding of the events that foreshadowed the offenses of the recent past helps us to acknowledge our shared responsibility for past mistakes. Only in this way can we fully participate in building a viable interfaith community. By confessing our past prejudices, forgiving the hate and prejudice we have experienced, and participating in community interfaith dialogue, we can all help advance the cause of global understanding and peace.

Pockets of Social Pressure

A few US communities have expressed concern about Muslim pressure to conform to the social or religious customs of Islam. Shari'ah or Islamic law seems to be the main issue. Shari'ah law is a shorthand expression for a body of legal rulings, judgments, and opinions that have been collected over many centuries. It covers a broad array of topics, ranging from ritual practice to criminal law, personal status, family law, commercial and transactional law, international law, and constitutional law.[5]

The area of Shari'ah law that guides personal and community faith and devotion is fully protected by the Bill of Rights. Outside the home and place of worship, however, religious regulations and practice of any and all religious groups have no authority. This long-established separation of church and state in American common life guarantees freedom of expression to people of every religious position.

Thus Shari'ah law as it relates to religion can never be written into American statutes. However, certain Islamic values may influence the writing of law through the normal legislative process. Over the generations, this has been the American way. Diverse values originating in cultures across the world have blended into the great multiethnic mural of our strong, integrated democracy.

Seeking Common Ground

Christians and Jews frequently cooperate in multi-faith efforts, especially when it comes to creating a wholesome community environment for families. All faithful parents desire a nurturing environment for their children. So it makes sense to work together for strong public education, improved police protection, and community recreational opportunities for our youth. Including Muslim parents in these efforts would not only make it more likely that faithful people will succeed in their attempt to strengthen the community, but it would also provide a point of contact for Muslims. The ultimate benefit would likely be the discovery that we have much in common, allowing our trust to build and the reality of God's love to overshadow our separateness.

The openness of the American experience has had a leavening influence around the world. There is a similar opportunity for American Muslim groups today to have an effective moderating influence on international Muslim policy. It is quite possible that true support and collegiality with Muslims could result in a strong social base here as well as stronger understanding and influence in international centers of Islamic policy development. Internationally recognized Muslim scholar Tariq Ramadan, writing in his book *Western Muslims and the Future of Islam* says, "Western Muslims will play a decisive role in the evolution of Islam worldwide because of the nature and complexity of the challenges they face."[6]

Collective witness has the potential to touch and restore hurting individuals in our communities, while adding enthusiastic new believers to our congregations as they see a growing sense of moral integrity in our communities. In the process, people of local congregations will quietly bear witness to their Muslim neighbors in a pattern of acceptance, love, and mutual service. As these neighbors are touched and served, their witness will reverberate around the world through the messages they communicate to family and friends located across the globe. The ultimate result of implementing a neighborhood witness gives voice, touch, and spiritual clarity to the healing call of Jesus to love God and love our neighbors as ourselves.

The Support Group Path from Faith to Service

It cannot be overemphasized that a community mission effort needs the total deployment of all active people of the congregation. All members should be involved according to their emerging levels of commitment and their unique capabilities and limitations. But specifically, how can we put our faith into service?

As the great English reformer John Wesley made clear, we discover our commitment to God within ourselves, but it is supported through the sensitive encouragement of spiritual nurture and accountability groups within the congregation. Through that support, each person in the community is equipped to become actively involved.

I only learned the theological origin of the small-group movement when, after our move to Bethlehem, my wife and I joined a vital United Methodist congregation. We soon learned that John Wesley had given the church a very practical teaching, which he called Christian conferencing. Wesley pointed out the psychologically sound reality that the burdens of discipleship need to be shared with a support group of like-minded committed believers. Without a common vision of God's call to discipleship, it is difficult to continue as a creative Christian serving the needs of a troubled world. The Wesley brothers, John and Charles, organized their followers into groups who gathered frequently for prayer, mutual encouragement, and support.

In recent years, the small-support-group concept has been broadly adopted in many churches and in the business community. Today there is the technology to vastly increase the effectiveness of the Christian conferencing group process. The methods employed for regular volunteer contact in the final twelve months of the 2008 presidential election illustrate the incredible power of electronic communication with large numbers of volunteers.

The congregation with whom I worship sends out via e-mail a daily devotional thought, a prayer list noting illness and concerns within the congregation, and a weekly message from the pastor. This is another illustration of the vast potential to harness congregational involvement. Christian conferencing has only touched the surface of its potential for support and guidance of community mission volunteers.

Technology, however, will not substitute for a regular time of face-to-face sharing of concerns. As the trust level of the group grows, there is also great value in regular occasions to affirm each other in humble confession and group prayer. In these small, reflective opportunities of Christian conferencing, the group as a unit is able to move beyond the typical limits of a self-help group and discover how to listen for the counsel of God. The benefits vary, but they often include:

- Inspiring individual members to boldly witness their faith through word and deed
- Clarifying community concerns with an ongoing sense of how to proceed
- Finding group wisdom for facing difficult community challenges
- Discerning whether to take action, refer to others, or simply to pray, wait, and see
- Determining new areas of service to be courageously explored and undertaken
- Gaining perception of how to maximize individual and/or group effectiveness
- Gaining vision for supporting Muslim or other minority needs in the community

While not neglecting the regular use of the other means of God's grace in worship, including prayer, fasting, and Bible study, Christian conferencing enables individuals to receive the spiritual power, guidance, and opportunity needed as instruments of God in community transformation. Such groups develop the spiritual and emotional capacity to respond to common issues with a humble but confident witness to the power of God.

There is an urgent need across denominational lines to challenge and equip our people to fully understand God's clear expectation for us to be committed disciples. The second chapter of the letter of James argues this issue carefully and then sharply concludes with two stern points: "Faith by itself, if it has no works, is dead" (James 2:17), and "You believe that God is one; you do well. Even the demons believe—and shudder" (James 2:19).

The Apostle Paul also deals with the faith/works nexus in his brief summary in Ephesians:

> For by grace you have been saved through faith, and this is not your own doing; it is the gift of God—not the result of works, so that no one may boast. For we are what he has made us, created in Christ Jesus for good works, which God prepared beforehand to be our way of life. (Ephesians 2:8–10)

We have been made in Christ Jesus, who in life, death, and resurrection gives us salvation *from* the pattern of this world *into* the new way he modeled: the way of the narrow door, the way that turns the other cheek, and the strange way that loves both neighbor and enemy as one loves themselves (Luke 1:77–79; 6:28–35; 13:24; Matthew 5:43–48).

The Exciting, Everyday Tasks of Sharing Faith through Love

When we pool information from our routine contacts as an active witnessing body, we learn about needs in the community. We may discover problems in the school system, dangerous playgrounds, the presence of homeless people, or youth who have no place to gather and no one who cares about them. We may notice potential pockets of hate and situations of abuse. We also learn how and when to speak up, what community meetings to attend, and with what community service organizations we can partner in our social ministry.

In the natural process of sensitive mission engagement on a day-to-day basis, we live with a double agenda. Our lives in the community are the same as everyone else's life, except for the ever-present, quiet awareness that we are also there as agents of God's love. Our witness is rarely intrusive or confrontational; rather, it is highly aware, supportive of people and their needs, and gently available as an agent of reconciling love. As specific concerns appear, we share them with our Christian conferencing group. The group can then prayerfully consider a response.

Whether offering cheerful greetings, picking up a piece of trash, comforting a crying child, or spending an extra five minutes speaking with a homeless person, the task is the same and yet always a bit different. Policemen on their beats are sensitive to law and order. As people of faith, we "patrol" our communities, sensitive to need and pain.

Since we are especially interested in Muslims (and others who may be marginalized or exploited), we will at times go out of our way to make those contacts. In most cases, we will find that Muslims are interested in the same community goals as other caring citizens. In general, they will eagerly partner with us in our overarching purpose of strengthening our community as a place of social health and peace.

By organizing community-support activity, we can often quietly neutralize hate-group activity. Where our collective support groups are insufficient for ending destructive influences, we can appeal to local police and other community organizations. Together with other faith groups and support agencies, we are in a strong position to end hateful actions and affirm the interfaith witness of the larger community. Such occasions of cooperation are an opportune time to establish a community-wide, interfaith dialogue.

In recent years, interfaith dialogue has been effective in bridging misunderstanding and binding communities together for a greater common purpose. An experienced, local church conferencing group will have the spiritual strength and organizational skill to spearhead the organization of a community action effort. This is another advantage of such accountability structures. Unlike church boards and committees that have an organizational agenda, members of the Christian conferencing groups are primarily the church's eyes and ears focused on human need, always ready in the spirit of Jesus to offer help and love as the occasion may require. As the result of that gentle outreach, they add new members to their group and build and strengthen their community.

The Painful Process of Change

To introduce this awareness of full Christian involvement into the life of a congregation is a challenging endeavor, one that can be accomplished only with prayerful, divine support and patient determination. As a pastor once remarked, changing the culture and direction of an established congregation is like convincing a two-year-old mare to leave a burning barn or a two-year-old boy to come in for a nap and leave the first snowfall he has ever seen. After all, religious faith and custom are a source of people's security. To even suggest that there is a better way of "being the church" than the way it has been done over the total memory of a congregation may seem like heresy. Those who are pastors and church leaders should not forget the tender touch, the listening ear, the intimate fellowship of prayer and study, and the call to "come away and rest a while" that all speak of the incarnating touch of Jesus, which is the church's soul.[7]

We are in a critical time of social stress and transition. Our nation is presently the one strong democracy with many pockets of vibrant Christian faith. We who see a better way should seek the face of God and then patiently practice and promote the lifestyle pattern of Jesus, expressing love in all our community contacts. In all seasons, amid concerns of every sort, let us dare to be patiently, persistently, and courageously obedient.

Afterword

Expressing the Love of God
through World Mission

Terrorists try to inspire a sense of estrangement and hatred among people. But the Bible tells us to love our neighbors (including our enemies) as ourselves, and Jesus calls us to enter into the world and love others as he loved us. The opportunity for creative, cross-cultural witness with Islam is greater than at any other time in history. There are dozens of effective ways to participate in meeting the physical, emotional, and spiritual needs of people in our communities and around the globe. Each one has the potential to build cooperation between Christians and Muslims, and a few are listed here.

Habitat for Humanity is a well-tested means of responding to people's urgent need for adequate shelter. It offers not only a gift, but also direct involvement by the families who participate in the building of their own new homes. Habitat builds houses for families around the world. It does this through the use of short-term volunteer groups from various local communities who supply their labor in partnership with the family members who will own the house.

In August 2008, Habitat for Humanity International partnered with the Islamic Society of North America and representatives of Jewish and Christian organizations to build awareness of poverty housing. Jonathan Reckford, CEO of Habitat, was a guest speaker at the annual convention of the Islamic Society in Columbus, Ohio. In his presentation he said, "All three monotheistic faiths share a call to serve the poor among us. In the case of Habitat for Humanity, an effort to answer that call created a global house-building organization that empowers families to overcome poverty through shelter."

In 2000, Habitat built its 100,000th house (in New York City) and its 100,001st house (in Plains, Georgia). In 2005, Habitat dedicated its 200,000th house (in Knoxville, Tennessee) and its 200,001st house (in Kanyakumari, India). In November 2008, Habitat dedicated its 300,000th house (in Naples, Florida) and its 300,001st house (in Zacapa, Guatemala). www.Habitat.org

Mercy Ships is an especially creative medical mission reaching desperately needy people on three continents. This mission has fully equipped hospitals on board ships that travel to ports where medical practices are limited and still primitive. As in the time of Jesus, people of all ethnic and religious backgrounds carry their needy for miles across the countryside to receive compassion and healing. One summer when my wife and I were serving in a teaching mission at the Lithuanian Christian College, one of the hospital ships was there in the port of Klaipeda. We were invited to visit the ship with some of our students. It was an exciting tour. They do incredible cross-cultural work of compassion. www.mercyships.org

LifeWind International, one of the most creative mission developments in recent years, is modeled closely on the ministry of Jesus. Community Health Evangelism (CHE) begins with a sensitive evaluation of the needs of a local community, whether sanitation, nutrition, clinical, or vocational, and then tries to address those needs. www.lifewind.org

International Rescue Committee helps those who are victims of the two recent wars in the Middle East, which have left thousands homeless and, in some cases, stateless. Children have been orphaned, crippled, and left without a home, adequate medical attention, and education. This organization works in the Middle East and in other desperately needy locations. Their website is very effective in describing their work and making clear how volunteers can participate. www.theirc.org

US Committee for Refugees and Immigrants aids some of the over seven thousand unaccompanied immigrant children who arrive in the United States each year without local contacts or resources. Many are fleeing from domestic violence, gang violence, human trafficking, and poverty. There is a great need for mentors and legal counsel. www. refugees.org

A Word of Accommodation

A special word to those who would genuinely like to be personally involved but find that other obligations make it impossible. Depending on where you are in the cycle of life, here are some alternative considerations to take seriously:

- *Student summer mission service* is available for older high school students and college students.
- *Extended vacations* of four to eight weeks give students time to include a short-term mission trip during part of the time away from school.
- *Retirement adventures* allow extended mission commitments of one to three years as well as summer short-term mission trips of two to eight weeks.

Since retirement, my wife and I have enjoyed a two-year mission experience as well as five short-term summer opportunities in Europe, Asia, and Africa. Whatever your situation, you will find true fulfillment in useful involvement. You may best serve by starting a new community outreach ministry in your local church or joining one that is already there. If you are open, God can startle you awake to the new adventure. There you can experience the "high" of spiritual joy.

As we each discover our part as a participant in the spiritual life of our community, others will be blessed, and we may discover that we have received the richest blessing of all. For practical guidance in getting involved in mission work, contact your denominational mission coordinator, Youth for Christ International, or World Vision.

May God bless your response to the high calling of the One who invested in you.

Timeline

The Life and Ministry
of the Prophet Muhammad

570 CE   Birth of Muhammad (Year of the Elephant); Muhammad's father dies before Muhammad is born.

570–573   Muhammad's mother Amina entrusts baby Muhammad to a Bedouin wet nurse so he will develop a good Arabic dialect and manners.

573   Muhammad is returned to his mother, who soon dies, leaving Muhammad with his grandfather.

580   The death of Abdul Muttalib, Muhammad's paternal grandfather and dear companion.

583   Muhammad joins the family of his uncle, Abu Talib; due to poverty, he becomes a shepherd.

594   Muhammad becomes manager of Lady Khadija's trade caravan business with Syria.

595	Lady Khadija proposes marriage; she and Muhammad have six children (four girls and two boys).
610	The first revelation to Muhammad by angel Gabriel in a cave on Mt. Hira.
613	Muhammad's first invitation to the general public to accept faith in the one true God.
617	Meccan leaders impose a social boycott on Muhammad and all followers of the one God.
619	The year of sadness; both Khadija and uncle Abu Talib die.
620	The Night Journey to Jerusalem.
621	The first pledge at Aqaba by interested converts from Medina.
622	In response to persecution, seventy Muslim families leave Mecca and move to Medina; later in the fall, Muhammad and Abu Bakr leave Mecca during the night and make the Hijra (migration) to Medina; this marks the official beginning of the Islamic calendar.
624	Battle of Badr, a major Muslim victory over the attacking Meccan force.
625	Battle of Uhud, the massacre of seventy Muslims under siege from a Meccan attack.

627	Muslims soundly defeat the Meccan army in the Battle of the Trench.
628	Truce of Hudaybiya, a high point of spiritual victory for Muhammad and his followers.
629	Muhammad performs the pilgrimage (Hajj) to the Ka'ba in Mecca.
630	Muhammad marches on Mecca with a large force; Muhammad and his forces enter the city and peacefully take it in the name of Islam.
632	Farewell pilgrimage to Mecca.
632	Death of Muhammad.

Islam and the Middle East After Muhammad

632–634	Muhammad's friend Abu Bakr serves as the first caliph.
634–644	Caliphate of Muhammad's friend Umar. His armies invade Iraq, Syria, and Egypt; in 638, his army conquers Jerusalem and they go on to defeat the Persian Empire.
644	Umar is assassinated; before dying, he appoints a Shura, or electoral committee, to choose the third caliph; they choose Uthman, Muhammad's son-in-law.

644–650   Caliph Uthman's armies conquer Cyprus and Tripoli and set up rule in Iran and Afghanistan.

656   Caliph Uthman is assassinated by malcontent Muslim soldiers; Muhammad's cousin and son-in-law, Ali ibn Abu Talib, becomes caliph.

661   Caliph Ali is murdered by a dissident; two major branches of Islam have developed: Sunni Islam and Shiite Islam reflect two approaches to political rule; Shiites believe Muhammad's charisma (spiritual and political guidance) was continued in the bloodline of Ali and his descendants; the Shiite imams believe in the continued guidance from the final imam, and tradition maintains that he will return as the mahadi to usher in the Day of Judgment. About 20 percent of Muslims, mostly from Iran and southern Lebanon, are Shiites; the other 80 percent are Sunnis, for whom selection of leaders takes place through representatives of the people. Both Sunnis and Shiites are considered orthodox and moderate.

661–680   Muawiyah, a relative of Uthman, is caliph.

680–685   Muawiyah dies; a second civil war starts between his son Yazid and Ali's second son Husayn, Muhammad's grandson. Followers of Ali become the Shiite minority. Husayn sets out with a small band and is martyred, finalizing the division between the Sunnis and Shiites.

691   The Dome of the Rock is completed in Jerusalem.

705–717   Caliphate of al-Walid. Muslim armies continue the conquest of North Africa and establish a kingdom in Spain.

717–720   Caliphate of Umar II, the first caliph to encourage conversion to Islam. He tries to implement some of the ideals of the religious movement formed by Muhammad.

732   The Battle of Poitiers; Charles Martel defeats a small raiding party of Spanish Muslims.

756   Muslim Spain secedes and sets up an independent kingdom under the leadership of Umayyad refugees.

786–809   Caliphate of Harun al-Rashid. The zenith of Abbasid power leads a great cultural renaissance in Baghdad; in addition to patronizing scholarship, science, and the arts, the caliph also encourages the study of *fiqh* to enable the formation of a coherent body of Islamic law (Shari'ah).

935   From this point, the caliphs no longer wield temporal power but retain merely a symbolic authority; real power now resides with the local rulers.

1099   Crusaders conquer Jerusalem and establish crusader states in Palestine, Anatolia, and Syria.

1187   Saladin defeats the crusaders at the Battle of Hattin and restores Jerusalem to Islam.

1224–1391   The Golden Mongol horde rules the lands north of the Caspian and Black Seas and converts to Islam.

1326–1359	Orkhan establishes an independent Ottoman state, with its capital at Brusa, which dominates the declining Byzantine Empire.
1412–1492	The Islamic Kingdom of Al-Andalus thrives in Spain with Muslim, Jewish, and Christian citizens and leaders.
1492	The Muslim Kingdom of Granada in Spain is conquered by the Catholic monarchs Ferdinand and Isabella. Arabs and Jews are subjected to the inquisition; when driven out of Spain, they are sheltered by the Ottoman Empire.
1502–1566	Ismail, head of the Safavid Sufi Order, conquers Iran, where he establishes Shiism, which follows the twelfth imam, as the official religion of Iran.
1520–1566	Suleiman, known in the West as the Magnificent, expands the Ottoman Empire.
1543	The Ottomans subjugate Hungary.
1560–1605	Akbar is the emperor of Mughal India, which reaches the zenith of its power; Akbar fosters Hindu-Muslim cooperation and conquers territory in south India.
1627–1658	Shah Jihan rules the Mughal Empire and builds the Taj Mahal.
1699	Treaty of Carlowicz cedes Ottoman Hungary to Austria, the first major Ottoman reversal.

1739   Nadir Shah sacks Delhi and puts an end to effective Mughal rule in India; Hindus, Sikhs, and Afghans compete for power.

1774   The Ottomans are defeated by the Russians and lose the Crimea; the Tsar becomes the "protector" of Orthodox Christians in Ottoman lands.

1860–1861   After a massacre of Christians by Druze rebels in Lebanon, the French demand that Lebanon becomes an autonomous province with a French governor.

1894   Ten thousand to twenty thousand Armenian revolutionaries against Ottoman rule are massacred.

The Evolution of Terrorist Ideology and Activity

1096–1218   The Crusades, a series of wars that destabilizes much of Europe, the Middle East, and North Africa, are launched by the Roman Catholic hierarchy to reclaim the city of Jerusalem and restore Rome's dominance over the eastern branch of Christendom; they discredit Western morality and spiritual integrity.

1492   Queen Isabella orders the Spanish Inquisition, the suppression and torture of Muslims and Jews justified by an ecclesiastical court in Roman Catholic Spain; this is an attempt at forced conversion.

1780–1790   Muhammad ibn Abd al-Wahhab joins forces with Arabic chieftain Ibn Al-Sa'ud and promotes a radical interpretation of Islam by distorting texts of the Qur'an, which depends on a Berber cultural approach to Islamic interpretation, using terror to gain power. Wahhab ideology in various forms has been behind the terror activity since this time; Osama bin Laden is a product of the Wahhab education system in Saudi Arabia.

1867   The formation of an Islamic Madrassa (school) and seminary in Deoband, India; the focus is on strict instruction in spiritual and moral Muslim teaching; by the end of the twentieth century, the leadership of the Afghanistan Taliban receive their training at what is now Deoband University.

1897   First Zionist conference held in Basel; the ultimate aim is to create a Jewish state in the Ottoman province of Palestine; This is the beginning of the Palestinian/Israeli crisis.

1901   Oil discovered in Iran; in an example of Western imperialism, concession is given to the British.

1914–1918   First World War; Britain declares Egypt a protectorate; British and Russian troops occupy Iran: the early stages of Western colonialism in the Middle East.

1917   Balfour Declaration formally gives British support to the creation of a Jewish homeland in Palestine.

1919 The Allies provide a US, English, and French naval escort as the Greek military invades Turkey in violation of the Mudros Accord with Turkey, agreed to on May 30, 1918; the Greeks move into central Turkey with a terrible loss of Christian and Muslim civilian life. The Allies abandon the Greek army and declare neutrality; the Turkish army drives the invaders back to the sea.

1919–20 The Versailles Peace Assembly divides the Ottoman North African provinces between the British and French in the wake of the German/Ottoman defeat in WWI, in spite of the fact that the British had promised North African Arabs independence in exchange for their Allied support during the war.

1922 Egypt is granted formal independence, yet Britain retains control of the Egyptian defense, foreign policy, and the Sudan.

1928 Hassan al Banna establishes The Muslim Brotherhood in Egypt, which focuses on restoring the purity of the original tenets of Muslim thought and practice; it supports a period of terror in its reform effort in Egypt; recently the Brotherhood has condemned the use of terror and distanced itself from the 9/11 attack.

1947 The UN General Assembly passes Resolution 181 on November 29; this establishes a three-part division of Palestine: an Israel free state, an independent Arab state, and an International Zone around Jerusalem. Each party wants more and rejects the Resolution.

1948   British forces leave Palestine on May 18 with no international agreement to solve the tension and uncertainty created by the failure of Resolution 181. Local Jewish leadership immediately moves into the power vacuum created by UN inactivity and the British departure and declares Israel an independent state. US President Harry Truman unilaterally acknowledges Israel's independence; the Arab nations attack Israel and are quickly defeated. Israel gains 30 percent more Palestinian territory than originally allocated by Resolution 181; Arabs flee from their homes in the newly enlarged Israeli state and are subsequently segregated to the relocation camps in Palestine, where many remain.

1951–1953   Muhammad Musaddiq and the National Front of Iran nationalize Iranian oil; the Shah flees Iran but is later returned to power, overthrowing a democratically elected Iranian leader in a coup organized by the CIA and British intelligence. New agreements are then made with Iran by European oil companies.

1967   The Six-Day War between Israel and its Arab neighbors; Israeli victory and humiliating Arab defeat leads to a Muslim revival throughout the Middle East.

1978–1979   The Iranian Revolution results in Ayatollah Khomeini becoming the Supreme Faqih of the Shiite Islamic Republic.

1979–1981   American are held hostage in the United States embassy in Tehran.

1987   Intifada, a popular Palestinian uprising in protest against the Israeli occupation of the West Bank and the Gaza Strip; Hamas enters the fray against Israel as well as against the PLO.

1990–1991   Saddam Hussein, secularist ruler of Iraq, invades Kuwait; the United States and its Western and Middle Eastern allies launch Operation Desert Storm. The United States uses Saudi Arabia as a staging area for its military effort; Osama bin Laden is infuriated that infidels occupy the holy land of the Prophet.

1992–1999   Serbian and Croatian nationalists systematically kill Muslims and force the Muslim inhabitants of Bosnia and Kosovo to leave their homes.

1993   Oslo Peace Accord.

1994   Following the assassination of twenty-nine Muslims in a Hebron mosque by Jewish extremists, Hamas suicide bombers attack Jewish civilians in Israel; The Israel/Palestine conflict continues to the present.

2001   September 11 al Qaeda attack: New York World Trade Center, Pentagon, and Pennsylvania plane crash.

2001–   Numerous terrorist incidents, including the foiled
present   American Airlines shoe bomb in December 2001 and foiled New York Times Square SUV bomb in May 2010.

Notes

Chapter One

1. Merton, *New Seeds of Contemplation*, 107.
2. Knight and Murphy, "Correspondence: The Sources of Terrorism," 192.
3. Lawrence, ed., *Messages to the World: The Statements of Osama Bin Laden*, 105.
4. Kersten, "Airport Taxi Flap About Alcohol Has Deeper Significance," B1.
5. Ibid.
6. Blair, "Making Muslim Integration Work," Opinion Page.
7. For Muslims' view on contemporary issues, see the Gallup Poll results in Esposito and Mogahed, *Who Speaks for Islam?: What a Billion Muslims Really Think*.

Chapter Two

1. See the genealogy of Mary in Luke, where it is assumed that Heli is Joseph's father-in-law. This explains the totally different genealogy from Jesus to David found in Matthew, where the legal listing of Joseph's genealogy is given.
2. Wagner, *Opening the Qur'an: Introducing Islam's Holy Book*, 21.

3. Lawrence, ed., *Messages to the World: The Statements of Osama Bin Laden* "Are We Safe? Islam, the Long Gray Line."
4. Dakake, "Some Misappropriation of Quranic Verses."
5. Wagner, 21.
6. Uzunoglu, trans., *The Glorious Qur'an: With English Translation and Commentary*, 282.
7. Additional information and the text of the letter can be found at the official website of A Common Word.

Section II Introduction

Note: The primary general resource for all material on the life of the Prophet Muhammad is Ishaq, *The Life of Muhammad: a Translation of Ishāq's "Sīrat Rasūl Allāh."*

1. Genesis 12–25 records the life and evolving monotheistic vision of Abram, whose name is changed to Abraham in Genesis 17:5. He is referred to throughout the First Testament and in the Gospels of Matthew and John as well as in Romans, Galatians, Hebrews, and James. Abraham is also prominent in the Qur'an, appearing in twenty of the Qur'an Surahs (chapters). A significant prayer of Abraham is quoted in Surah 2:128: "O our Lord! Make us submitters to You! And raise from among our offspring a community which will be submitters to You. Show us our ways of worship, and relent toward us. You are indeed the Forgiving, the Merciful." Note: it is significant that the noun "submitter" is the English translation of the Arabic term *Muslim*.

2. Cahill, *The Gifts of the Jews: How a Tribe of Desert Nomads Changed the Way Everyone Thinks and Feels*, 3. This reference relates to a period in history prior to Judaism. I have used the terms "the vision of Abraham" and "Abrahamic vision" where Cahill has used "the Jews." The monotheistic vision of Abraham was shared with other Semitic groups, although we see the influence of the vision more clearly later in what becomes Jewish culture.

Chapter Three

1. Wagner, *Opening the Qur'an: Introducing Islam's Holy Book*, 5.
2. Smith, *The World's Religions: Our Great Wisdom Traditions*, 11.
3. Ishaq, *The Life of Muhammad: a Translation of Ishāq's "Sīrat Rasūl Allāh."* 45.
4. Armstrong, *Muhammad: a Biography of the Prophet*, 62.
5. Cragg, *The Call of the Minaret*, 66.

Chapter Four

1. Ishaq, *The Life of Muhammad: a Translation of Ishāq's "Sīrat Rasūl Allāh."* 81.
2. Dirks, *Understanding Islam*, 114.
3. Bettenson, ed., *Documents of the Christian Church*, 125ff.
4. Ishaq, 86.

Chapter Five

1. Dirks, *Understanding Islam*, 130.
2. Ishaq, *The Life of Muhammad: a Translation of Ishāq's "Sīrat Rasūl Allāh."* 106.
3. Armstrong, *Muhammad: a Biography of the Prophet*, 84.
4. Ishaq, 107.
5. Ibid., 118.
6. Armstrong, 126.
7. Ishaq, 159.
8. Ibid., 172–3.
9. Ibid., 191.
10. Ibid., 183.
11. Ibid., 199.
12. Ibid., 204.
13. Ibid., 208.

Chapter Six

1. Ishaq, *The Life of Muhammad: a Translation of Ishāq's "Sīrat Rasūl Allāh."* 228.

2. Ibid., 236.
3. Ibid., 240.
4. Ibid., 258. A Qur'an text appears to respond to this bitter quarrel: Surah 2:135–6.

Chapter Seven

1. Ishaq, *The Life of Muhammad: a Translation of Ishāq's "Sīrat Rasūl Allāh."* 337–9.
2. Ibid., 317.
3. Ibid., 361.
4. Ibid., 367–369.
5. Ibid., 370.
6. Ibid., 372.
7. Ibid., 450.
8. Armstrong, *Muhammad: a Biography of the Prophet*, 186.
9. Ishaq, 453.
10. Ibid., 460.
11. Armstrong, 206.

Chapter Eight

1. Armstrong, *Muhammad: a Biography of the Prophet*, 212.
2. Ishaq, *The Life of Muhammad: a Translation of Ishāq's "Sīrat Rasūl Allāh."* 500.
3. Armstrong, 217.
4. Ibid., 220.
5. Ibid., 221.
6. Ishaq, 507.
7. Nasr, *The Heart of Islam: Enduring Values for Humanity*, 237.
8. Armstrong, 243.
9. Ishaq, 553.
10. Cragg, *The Qur'an and the West*, 158.
11. Ishaq, 679.
12. Armstrong, 258.

Chapter Nine

1. Cragg, *The Qur'an and the West*, 156.
2. Armstrong, *Muhammad: a Biography of the Prophet*, 250.
3. Hitti, *The Arabs: A Short History*, 117.
4. Ibid., 119–120.
5. Ibid., 120.
6. For additional information about Islamic civilization in Spain see "Muslim Spain."
7. Fisher, *The Middle East, a History*, 172.
8. Ibid., 174.
9. Ibid., 202.
10. Ibid., 203.
11. Ibid., 206.

Chapter Ten

1. "Worldview" refers to the inner personal sense that emerges out of culture and education and gives order and coherence to life in terms of a personal sense of identity, meaning, and purpose.
2. Abou El Fadl, *The Great Theft: Wrestling Islam from the Extremists*, 44–47.
3. Ibid., 40
4. *CRS Report for Congress*, 1–12.
5. Abou El Fadl, 3–4.
6. Ibid., 5–6.
7. In Qur'an 3:8, Wahhab is the last of the 99 names used for God in the Qur'an and means all-bestowing or liberal giver. Having this name may have influenced Wahhab's acceptance by the Bedouin and Arabic community.
8. Abou El Fadl, 56.
9. Ibid., 45–55.
10. Schwartz, *The Two Faces of Islam: Saudi Fundamentalism and Its Role in Terrorism*, 110.
11. Ibid., 111.
12. Ibid., 113.
13. Lawrence, ed., *Messages to the World: The Statements of Osama Bin Laden*, 104.

14. Akbar, "There Is More Going On," 9.
15. *CRS Report for Congress*, 11–12.
16. "Oral History Interview with Fraser Wilkins."
17. John, "Behind the Balfour Declaration: Britain's Great War Pledge to Lord Rothchild," 4:389.
18. Ibid.
19. Ibid.
20. The Tragedy of the SS *St. Louis*.
21. "Oral History Interview with Fraser Wilkins."
22. As we will discuss later in the book, President Truman's decision may indirectly have cost us the tragedy of 9/11.
23. Lawrence, ed., *Messages to the World: The Statements of Osama Bin Laden*, 105.

Section IV Introduction

1. Pope Paul VI, "Nostra Aetate: Declaration on the Relation of the Church to Non-Christian Religions."
2. Oates, "Words Fail, Memory Blurs, Life Wins," A10.
3. Weigel, "The War Against Jihadism," 49.

Chapter Eleven

1. *The Fog of War: Eleven Lessons from the Life of Robert S. McNamara*.
2. Frykholm, "An Interview with Ron Hansen."
3. Camp, *Mere Discipleship: Radical Christianity in a Rebellious World*, 57–58.

Chapter Twelve

1. Lawrence, ed., *Messages to the World: The Statements of Osama Bin Laden*, 167–168.
2. King Abdullah II, *The Amman Message*.
3. See the official website of A Common Word.
4. "A Christian Response to 'A Common Word Between Us and You.'"
5. Abou El Fadl, *The Great Theft: Wrestling Islam from the Extremists*, 149.

6. Ramadan, *Western Muslims and the Future of Islam*, 225.
7. Wilson, "Churches Now and in the Future: a 21st Century Babylonian Exile," 12.

Glossary

Adhan

Muslim call to prayer, five times a day

Allah

"The God"; the Arabic term used by Arab Christians and Muslims for God

akbar

the superlative of "to be great"; great beyond all comparison

ansari

helpers, or of the helpers; the inhabitants of Medina who aided Muhammad and those who emigrated from Mecca to Medina

Caliph

successor or supreme ruler; the title taken by those who followed Muhammad in the key leadership role

Dar al-Islam

the realm or place where Islam is in full control; in contrast to Dar al Harb, the place where Islam is not yet in control, or non-Muslim lands

dawah or Da'wah	literally "call"; God's call to people to become Muslim
dhimmi	the place or the status of being religiously free but living within specific limits set by a state governed by Shari'ah law
fatwa	a legal opinion delivered by an acknowledged Muslim legal authority
Five Pillars	ritual practices of Islam that provide Muslims moral guidance and an unceasing reminder of the centrality of Allah (God) in every aspect of human life
hadith	a collection of sayings and customs of the Prophet Muhammad; plural ahadith
Hajj	pilgrimage; the fifth Pillar of Islam; annual gathering of Muslims in Mecca at the Ka'ba
Hijrah	the migration from Mecca to a safe haven in Medina; the date of the Hijrah by Muhammad became the official date to start the Muslim calendar
intifada	uprising; literally a throwing off
Islam	the root meaning is peace or submission and signifies those who have surrendered their lives to Allah (God)

Jahiliyyah	age of ignorance; a state of ignorant, lawless paganism attributed to the early people of Arabia
jihad	the root meaning is endeavor or struggle; it is used in the sense of an inner effort to achieve spiritual purity or in a national effort to safeguard the integrity of the Muslim umma or community
jinn	dark, spiritual beings of the desert of Arabia; made of fire and smoke
Ka'ba	the cube-like structure in Mecca where the idols were kept and now the symbol to Muslims of the presence of God
kafir	unbeliever
Madrassa	a Muslim school for religious and perhaps also secular education
Mufti	a judge or a person qualified to give an authoritative opinion on Islamic law
Muslims	the followers of Islam
mushrikun	polytheists, idolaters
Night of Power	the night when Muhammad, meditating in the cave, was first confronted by the angel Gabriel and told to "recite" the initial words of the Qur'an

People of the Book	the phrase used in the Qur'an for Jews and Christians, those numbered with Muslims as monotheists
qibla	the point or direction that all Muslims face when praying, i.e. facing Mecca
Qur'an	the revealed words of Allah (God) given to Muhammad by the angel Gabriel
Quraysh	the tribal group of Mecca; Muhammad's tribe of origin
Ramadan	a month for prayer and reflection with fasting during the day; one of the five Pillars of Islam
Salat	the ritual prayer performed before God with the sacred movements of bowing, kneeling, and being prostrate before Allah (God) at five periods each day; one of the five Pillars of Islam
Shahadah	the sacred declaration of faith in Allah (God) and his Prophet Muhammad; this declaration is made when one formally enters the Muslim faith and at other sacred times; one of the five Pillars of Islam
Sawm	fasting; part of the Ramadan ritual practice
Shari'ah	the way; God's law as divinely presented in the Qur'an and Hadith

Surah	used in place of chapter for the names and numbers of each individual section in the Qur'an
Umma or Ummah	the unity of the entire community of Islam; also a modern Arabic term for "nation" involving the sense of a nation of the faithful
Zakat	the act of giving alms; one of the five Pillars of Islam

Bibliography

Abou El Fadl, Khaled. *The Great Theft: Wrestling Islam from the Extremists*. New York, NY: HarperOne, 2005.

Akbar, M. J. "There Is More Going On." *Fellowship* 70, no. 9-10 (2002).

"Are We Safe? Islam, the Long Gray Line." *60 Minutes*. CBS. September 30, 2001.

Armstrong, Karen. *Muhammad: a Biography of the Prophet*. San Francisco, CA: HarperSanFrancisco, 1992.

Bettenson, Henry, ed. *Documents of the Christian Church*. Galaxy ed. Vol. II. World's Classics. New York: Oxford University Press, 1947.

Blair, Tony. "Making Muslim Integration Work." *Wall Street Journal*, November 9, 2010.

Cahill, Thomas. *The Gifts of the Jews: How a Tribe of Desert Nomads Changed the Way Everyone Thinks and Feels*. New York: Doubleday, Anchor Books, 1998.

Camp, Lee C. *Mere Discipleship: Radical Christianity in a Rebellious World*. Grand Rapids MI: Brazos Press, 2003.

"A Christian Response to 'A Common Word Between Us and You'" Yale Center for Faith and Culture. http://www.yale.edu/faith/about/abou-volf.htm (accessed September 10, 2010).

"A Common Word Between Us and You." Muslim Clerics to The Pope and the Worldwide Christian Community. 2007. http://www.ammanmessage.com (accessed September 8, 2010).

Cragg, A. Kenneth. *The Call of the Minaret.* Oxford: Oneworld, 2003. Note: this Kenneth Cragg is a Bishop of the Church of England and an acclaimed author and scholar of Islam for over six decades and should not be confused with the author of this book.

Cragg, A. Kenneth. *The Qur'an and the West.* Washington, DC: Georgetown University Press, 2006.

Dakake, David. "Some Misappropriation of Quranic Verses." Islam Is The Religion Of Peace. http://www.religionofpeace.com/index_files/Page1006.htm (accessed September 08, 2010).

Dirks, Jerald F. *Understanding Islam.* Beltsville, MD: Amana Publications, 2003.

Esposito, John L., and Dalia Mogahed. *Who Speaks for Islam?: What a Billion Muslims Really Think.* New York, NY: Gallup Press, 2007.

Fisher, Sydney Nettleton. *The Middle East, a History.* New York: Knopf, 1959.

The Fog of War: Eleven Lessons from the Life of Robert S. McNamara. DVD. Directed by Errol Morris. US: Sony Pictures Classics, 2004.

Frykholm, Amy J. "An Interview with Ron Hansen." *The Christian Century,* August 12, 2008. http://www.religion-online.org/showarticle.asp?title=3577 (accessed September 8, 2010).

Hitti, Philip K. *The Arabs; a Short History.* Gateway ed. Princeton: Princeton Univ. Press, 1949.

Ishaq, Muhammad Ibn. *The Life of Muhammad: a Translation of Ishāq's "Sīrat Rasūl Allāh."* trans. Alfred Guillaume. Karachi: Oxford University Press, 2006.

John, Robert. "Behind the Balfour Declaration: Britain's Great War Pledge to Lord Rothchild." *The Journal of Historical Review* 6, no. 4: 389-450. http://www.vho.org/GB/Journals/JHR/6/4/John389-450 .html (accessed September 8, 2010).

Kersten, Katherine. "Airport Taxi Flap About Alcohol Has Deeper Significance." *Minneapolis Star Tribune*, October 26, 2006, sec. B.

King Abdullah II. *The Amman Message*. Amman, Jordan: Royal Aal Al-Bayt Institute for Islamic Thought, 2008. www.ammanmessage .com (accessed September 8, 2010).

Knight, Charles, and Melissa Murphy. "Correspondence: The Sources of Terrorism." *International Security* 28, no. 2, Fall 2003. http://www .comw.org/pda/fulltext/03knightmurphy.pdf (accessed October 6, 2010).

Lawrence, Bruce, ed. *Messages to the World: the Statements of Osama Bin Laden*. Translated by James Howarth. London: Verso, 2005.

Merton, Thomas. *New Seeds of Contemplation*. Boston: Shambhala, 2003.

"Muslim Spain." Si, Spain. http://www.sispain.org/english/history/ muslim.html (accessed May 23, 2007).

Nasr, Seyyed Hossein. *The Heart of Islam: Enduring Values for Humanity*. San Francisco: HarperSanFrancisco, 2002.

Oates, Joyce Carol. "Words Fail, Memory Blurs, Life Wins." *New York Times*, December 31, 2001.

The Official Website of A Common Word. http://www.acommonword .com/ (accessed September 10, 2010).

"Oral History Interview with Fraser Wilkins." Interview by Richard D. McKinzie. Harry S. Truman Library & Museum. http://www .trumanlibrary.org/oralhist/wilkins.htm (accessed September 8, 2010).

Pope Paul VI. "Nostra Aetate: Declaration on the Relation of the Church to Non-Christian Religions." The Holy See - Archive Documents

- of the II Vatican Council. http://www.vatican.va/archive/hist
_councils/ii_vatican_council/documents/vat-ii_decl_19651028
_nostra-aetate_en.html (accessed September 8, 2010).

Ramadan, Tariq. *Western Muslims and the Future of Islam.* New York: Oxford University Press, 2004.

Schwartz, Stephen. *The Two Faces of Islam: Saudi Fundamentalism and Its Role in Terrorism.* New York: Anchor Books, 2003.

Smith, Huston. *The World's Religions: Our Great Wisdom Traditions.* San Francisco: HarperSanFrancisco, 1991.

"The Tragedy of the SS *St. Louis.*" Jewish Virtual Library - Homepage. http://www.jewishvirtuallibrary.org/jsource/Holocaust/stlouis.html (accessed September 8, 2010).

US Congress. *CRS Report for Congress.* By Christopher M. Blanchard. Cong. Rept. RS21695. http://fpc.state.gov/documents/organization/81366. pdf (accessed September 8, 2010).

Uzunoglu, Nurettin, trans. *The Glorious Qur'an: With English Translation and Commentary.* 8th ed. Piscataway, NJ: 1-877-WHY-ISLAM, 2003.

Wagner, Walter H. *Opening the Qur'an: Introducing Islam's Holy Book.* Notre Dame, IN: University of Notre Dame Press, 2008.

Weigel, George. "The War Against Jihadism." *Newsweek,* January 26, 2008. http://www.newsweek.com/2008/01/26/the-war-against -jihadism.html (accessed September 8, 2010).

Wilson, Victor M. "Churches Now and in the Future: a 21st Century Babylonian Exile." *The Presbyterian Outlook* 190, no. 38 (November 17, 2008).

Additional Resources

American Islam: The Struggle for the Soul of a Religion, Paul M. Barrett

Is The Father of Jesus The God of Muhammad, Timothy George.

Building a Better Bridge: Muslims, Christians, and the Common Good, Michael Ipgrave, Editor.

Three Cups of Tea, Greg Mortensen and David Oliver Relin

What's Right With Islam Is What's Right With America, Feisal Abdul Rauf.

Glad News! God Loves You, My Muslim Friend, Samy Tanagho.

Center for Islamic Pluralism, www.islamicpluralism.org.

About the Author

The Reverend Doctor Kenneth B. Cragg (known as Blaine to his family and Ken to his friends) was raised among the fruit orchards of central Washington State. He served as an infantryman in the final stages of WWII in Germany. Dr. Cragg has degrees from the University of California at Berkeley, Princeton Theological Seminary, and Fuller Theological Seminary, and he has served more than fifty years as a clergyman and college professor. Ken and his wife, Willa, live in Kirkland Village, Bethlehem, Pennsylvania.

Dr. Cragg delights in travel and has participated in summer volunteer teaching assignments in Klaipeda, Lithuania; St. Petersburg, Russia; Qingdao, China; and Kigali, Rwanda. He has made trips through various parts of Europe as well as in Egypt, Israel, and Morocco. He has four children, ten grandchildren, and three great-grandchildren, as well as twelve foster children who were part of the family for various amounts of time.

The inspiration to write this book became a passion in the course of teaching world religion courses immediately after 9/11. He could find no text that honestly presented Islam and its essential distinction with the radical terrorists of al Qaeda.

Of greater concern was the confusion on the part of well-intentioned Christians who condemned Muslims en masse for al Qaeda's crimes, although they are clearly repudiated by the teaching and practice of faithful Muslims. Following the carnage at the World Trade Center and the Pentagon, there was disdain for American Muslims, whose countries of origin were also suffering deep wounds inflicted by the radical terror movement.

Thus the book comes out of an urgent desire to set the record straight and find common ground on which Christians and Muslims, despite serious theological differences, have cause to build a united front against terrorism, a critical threat to the faith and health of human civilization.

Index